Respecting Congregations

Respecting Congregations

Encouraging Congregations to Rediscover Their Truest Identity, Purpose, and Ministry

Clyde Ervine

WIPF & STOCK · Eugene, Oregon

RESPECTING CONGREGATIONS
Encouraging Congregations to Rediscover Their Truest Identity, Purpose, and Ministry

Copyright © 2025 Clyde Ervine. All rights reserved. Except for brief quotations in critical publications or reviews, no part of this book may be reproduced in any manner without prior written permission from the publisher. Write: Permissions, Wipf and Stock Publishers, 199 W. 8th Ave., Suite 3, Eugene, OR 97401.

Wipf & Stock
An Imprint of Wipf and Stock Publishers
199 W. 8th Ave., Suite 3
Eugene, OR 97401

www.wipfandstock.com

PAPERBACK ISBN: 979-8-3852-3063-1
HARDCOVER ISBN: 979-8-3852-3064-8
EBOOK ISBN: 979-8-3852-3065-5

VERSION NUMBER 05/20/25

Scripture quotations without notation are taken from Common Bible: New Revised Standard Version Bible, copyright © 1989 National Council of the Churches of Christ in the United States of America. Used by permission. All rights reserved worldwide.

Scripture quotations marked NIV are taken from the Holy Bible, New International Version®, NIV®. Copyright © 2011 by Biblica, Inc.™ Used by permission of Zondervan. All rights reserved worldwide. www.zondervan.com

Scripture quotations marked KJV are taken from The Authorized (King James) Version. Rights in the Authorized Version in the United Kingdom are vested in the Crown. Reproduced by permission of the Crown's patentee, Cambridge University Press.

Scripture quotations marked MSG are taken from THE MESSAGE, copyright © 1993, 2002, 2018 by Eugene H. Peterson. Used by permission of NavPress. All rights reserved. Represented by Tyndale House Publishers, Inc.

Dedicated to my late parents, Samuel and Josephine Ervine, who modeled for my siblings and me their joyful Christian faith, lived out in service to a congregation

Contents

Acknowledgments | ix
List of Abbreviations | xi
Introduction | xiii

1 Preliminary Musings on Respect | 1
2 The Bible's Respect for Congregations | 13
3 The Challenge Involved in Respecting Congregations | 39
4 Theological Respect for Congregations | 65
5 Respecting Congregational Ministry | 89

Epilogue | 119
Bibliography | 123

Acknowledgments

THE PERIL OF AUTHORING a book on respect is that those who know me know I don't always practice what I preach. For that, I ask forgiveness, not least from the church communities I served. When I recall my ministry among those five Canadian congregations—St. Andrew's in Sutton, Chippawa in Niagara Falls, St. Giles Kingsway in Toronto, Central in Hamilton, and Knox in St. Catharines—I smile with pleasure but also blush with embarrassment for all my blunders. I wish that I had known then what I think I know now! Among those who helped to shape my approach to congregational ministry, I mention Dr. Fred Rennie. As minister of St. John's Church, Cornwall, Ontario, Fred kindly oriented me to church life on my arrival in Canada from the UK and supervised my year as a student in that congregation. Another who modeled respectful ministry for me was Dr. Bill Adamson, whom I succeeded in 1991 as minister at St. Giles Kingsway Church, Toronto. I recall Bill's respectful request, sometime thereafter, that he and his wife Brenda return to worship in the congregation where he served for forty years. Bill also taught me respect for public worship. I also acknowledge my friend Dr. John Vissers, who welcomed me as a colleague when he was principal of Presbyterian College, Montreal, and later Knox College, Toronto, where he models for theological students a respect for the identity and integrity of the church.

There are others who, knowing my severe techno-peasant limits, helped get this book to the publisher; among them are Hannah Skelding, Rosemary Vysohlid, and especially Kate Unrau. I sincerely thank them for their patience. I thank the Reverend Marilyn Savage, a former student of mine who, on reading the chapters of this book, offered me good, gentle advice; I thank the Reverend Doug Schonberg who assisted me

Acknowledgments

with bibliographical details; and I thank the Reverend Bernie Skelding, my minister, for constant inspiration. Finally, I acknowledge Paul Hicks, my best friend for the last forty years. Paul enjoys and contributes generously to congregational life, but he also knows how flawed are the clergy who lead them!

List of Abbreviations

1 Cor	1 Corinthians	Isa	Isaiah
1 Kgs	1 Kings	Jas	James
1 Pet	1 Peter	Jer	Jeremiah
1 Sam	1 Samuel	KJV	King James Version
2 Cor	2 Corinthians	Lev	Leviticus
Col	Colossians	Matt	Matthew
Dan	Daniel	NIV	New International Version
Deut	Deuteronomy		
Eph	Ephesians	NRSV	New Revised Standard Version
Esth	Esther		
Exod	Exodus	Phil	Philippians
Gal	Galatians	Phlm	Philemon
Gen	Genesis	Ps	Psalm
GOCN	Gospel and Our Culture Network	Rev	Revelations
		Rom	Romans
Heb	Hebrews	1 Thess	1 Thessalonians

Introduction

I HAVE ALWAYS BEEN immersed in congregations. Raised in a Presbyterian congregation in Ireland, I was active in congregations during my university years in Scotland and England, after which I served as a minister in five Canadian Presbyterian congregations. But though congregations are almost always intriguing, I for some years left congregational ministry to teach at Presbyterian College, Montreal. While preparing students there to lead congregations, I shared with them some of what you will read in this book. Those who reveled in the intellectual challenge of theology found my material too applied; other students, I suspect, found it a relief after reading Karl Barth's *Church Dogmatics*.

My book sets out to address the currently stressed congregations of North America. A wide range of material offers "how-to" advice to those congregations; some of it is useful, but too much of it offers strategies to help congregations as organizations while bypassing, in part or in whole, theological reflection on congregations. Believing that congregations are crucial to the passing of the Christian faith from generation to generation, in this book, I urge congregational leaders to step back from congregational activity to ask these three questions: What is a congregation? What is a congregation for? What is essential to congregational ministry? Though congregations are free to make all sorts of optional local decisions, decisions that eventually lead each congregation to be unique, it is my conviction that a congregation will flourish if its leaders and members see their congregation as a community of Jesus's followers, with an identity, purpose, and pattern of ministry rooted in the New Testament. I believe that clarity and respect—about and for what God intends congregations to be and to do—can restore and reinvigorate them.

Introduction

As to what follows, I must admit that my congregational experience is limited, having mostly spent my life in British and Canadian mainline Protestant congregations, not in big-*E* Evangelical, Charismatic, Catholic, or American congregations. Here is an outline of what to expect as you read further:

- Chapter 1 introduces the topic of respect and what it means, and how respect shows up (or doesn't) in church and in congregational life.
- Chapter 2 looks briefly at what the Bible says about respect and then turns to trace in more detail the New Testament's respect for congregational identity.
- Chapter 3 reviews various strategies proposed since the 1960s to arrest the decline of North America's Protestant congregations and argues that those strategies often lack respect for the biblical identity of congregations as rehearsed in chapter 2.
- Chapter 4 outlines approvingly how recent missional theologians locate congregations within the Bible's narration of God's kingdom and mission, claiming that respect for that location can provide congregations with purpose, hope, and direction.
- Chapter 5 promotes respect for the New Testament's pattern for congregational ministry—gathering for Christian formation and scattering for Christian witness.
- The epilogue offers words of encouragement for discouraged leaders in a time of continuing congregational unraveling.

As I wrote the chapters outlined above, I often thought of a book titled *10 Habits for Effective Ministry: A Guide for Life-Giving Pastors,* by Lowell Erdahl, an American Lutheran bishop. Its wisdom supplemented the more analytical textbooks that students taking my congregational leadership course in seminary were assigned. I would like my book to be another such supplement, though I am haunted by a line that may come from the feisty Christopher Hitchens: "Everyone has a book within them, and in most cases that is where it should stay."

Before being ordained as a minister, I trained as a church historian—my doctorate focused on the nineteenth-century Church of England. Now retired, I have had more time to think and write, doing so as a generalist, not an academic specialist. However, I have added chapter footnotes, though aware that no footnote exists for some of the assertions I make!

Introduction

Far from seeking originality, I discuss the proposals made by church leaders and scholars to help North America's congregations, so many of which have declined over the last sixty years. My hope is to somehow get behind those proposals, some of them helpful, to wrestle with more fundamental questions about congregations in an effort to encourage clergy, seminary students, and lay congregational leaders to find fresh direction for their ministries.

The Canadian congregations that I served faced challenges similar to those faced by most North American congregations, challenges related to the collapse of Christendom and the emergence of what is now called a post-Christian era. Because I believe such challenges to be deeper than those assumed by many strategies being offered to help North American congregations succeed or at least survive, I have no easy answers. Inclined neither to simply carry on doing what congregations have traditionally done nor to latch on to every new "fix-it" strategy that comes along, I want to suggest that congregations slow down their ministries, resist the appeal of quick-fix changes, question the obsolete Christendom assumptions that have long shaped congregational identity and purpose, and instead seek and then respect the identity, purpose, and pattern of ministry offered to congregations by the New Testament.

But why use the lens of respect? The idea caught my attention as a child when my parents told me to pay attention to my teachers at school and to electricity at home, which in British homes is delivered at double the strength of that delivered to North American homes. If I initially linked respect to fear, I later learned as a young minister to think of respect more positively when, for example, I discussed with those about to be married why the word "respect" was used in the marriage liturgy. I recall one prospective bride, a petite blonde about to marry a man built like a night-club bouncer, who admitted she felt disrespected by her husband-to-be. We agreed that their wedding plans should be put on hold, but some weeks later, having been assured that they had worked things out, I officiated at their wedding. Six months later they parted. I underestimated the importance of respect.

Years later, while teaching at Presbyterian College, Montreal, I was still brooding on respect, for on recently reading what I wrote in my journal on October 31, 2004, I noted the idea of writing about respect. My interest at that point related to evaluating student sermons, in which I looked for evidence that the sermons respected the Bible as well as those who would

Introduction

hear them. Additionally, as I visited congregations in which students were placed for supervision, I found myself regularly noting either the presence or the absence of a culture of respect.

But if interested in respectful behavior *within* congregations, the core concern of my book is respect *for* congregations. For centuries, congregations enjoyed a settled, prominent, and prestigious place in North American society, reflected in their architecture. Their prominence and prestige meant that congregations rarely felt the need to work out why they existed. Times have changed! That being so, I call on today's congregations to carefully consider their identity, purpose, and priorities, clarified in the Bible's narration of God's mission, and commended by contemporary missional theologians. By doing this, congregations and their leaders can gain confidence to continue Christian ministry in tough times. My sense, however, is that too many congregations remain unaware of how theological reflection could help them, instead seeking a "fix-it" strategy or simply giving up. To help such, my modest-sized book sorts through the key insights of the missional theologians, to which I have added reflection on my own experience of congregational leadership.

Lastly, I confess that as a congregational leader, particularly in the early years, I ran around like a chicken with its head cut off. My leadership style was essentially reactive and unfocused. It took me decades to discover the importance of reflecting on and respecting what a congregation is, what its critical purpose is, and what its key ministry priorities ought to be. To all of that, I now turn.

1

Preliminary Musings on Respect

There was once an old man whose eyes blinked and whose hands trembled. When he ate, he clattered the silverware noisily, often missed his mouth with the spoon, and dribbled his food on the tablecloth. He lived with his son; but his son's wife didn't like it. "I can't have it," she told her husband; "it spoils my happiness."

One day the couple took the old man, sat him on a stool in the kitchen corner, and gave him his food in an earthenware bowl. From then on, that's where he always ate, wistfully looking over to the table. But his hands continued to tremble, causing the earthenware bowl to fall and to break. "If you're a pig," said his now angry daughter-in-law, "you must eat out of a trough." So, they made him a small wooden trough in which they placed his food.

The young couple had a four-year-old son on whom they doted. One evening, his dad noticed his young son playing with bits of wood and asked what he was doing. "I'm making a trough," he said, "to feed you and Mamma out of when I get big." The parents silently looked at each other, went to the corner, took the old man by the arm, led him back to the table, sat him in a comfortable chair, and gave him his food on a plate. From that time onward, there was no scolding when he clattered or spilled or broke things.

THIS FOLK TALE, PARAPHRASED from one published by the Grimm Brothers in 1812, warns us to think about how we act in front of others, especially children; illustrates the Golden Rule ("In everything do to others as you would have them do to you" [Matt 7:12]); and introduces the topic of respect—what it is and to whom it is due. This much is already clear: Respect has to do with how we see, evaluate, and treat other people—and everything else.

My particular interest is to look at congregations through a lens of respect, which means standing back from the details of their ministries to look at the assumptions that shape how we see and lead them. That said, respect is not an abstract issue for congregations; it is a daily challenge. For example, as a minister, I was often tempted to respect only those congregational members I deemed "useful" while dismissing those whom I didn't so deem. As for congregational members, because they disagree on issues large and small, they find it challenging to respect one another. I think, for example, of current contested views on sexuality.

But if respect *within* congregations matters (and I will touch on that from time to time), my key concern is to explore what respect *for* congregations entails and to ask why congregations are reluctant to take the time to respect or even recognize what God calls and equips congregations to be and to do. I say that because congregations often spend considerable time and energy on issues that stand at some distance from what the New Testament presents as central to their identity, purpose, and ministry. To take one example, it is not unknown for congregations to pursue a variety of tasks, some of them useful, but to ignore and thus disrespect the task Jesus clearly commanded his disciples to do: Go and make disciples.

WHAT IS RESPECT?

I begin by discussing what respect is and isn't, aware that the meaning of this now overused word is rather elusive. Most of us will have experienced disrespect in congregations and maybe even perpetuated it, yet disrespect is more than a lack of good manners. In her book *The Soul of Civility*, Alexandra Hudson calls for a revival of civility, which she says involves more than politeness. Politeness, she writes, "is a technique; it is decorum, mores, and etiquette [that] can be used for good or for ill depending on a person's inner motivation."[1] Civility, on the other hand, "is a disposition, a way of seeing others as being endowed with dignity and inherently valuable" that treats others "as intrinsically valuable and worthy of respect."[2] Hudson

---

1. Hudson, *Soul of Civility*, 13.
2. Hudson, *Soul of Civility*, 13.

Preliminary Musings on Respect

rightly sees that civility and respect overlap, for civility calls us to suppress our ego and our lust for power when interacting with others so that mutual respect, social cohesion, and civilized society can flourish.

But though Hudson differentiates between civility and politeness, she does not seem to differentiate between civility and respect. Civility, she says, is a disposition that, if cultivated, will make human interactions less abrasive and more positively pleasant. But as we shall see, respect is more complex. For a start, while respect will likely foster harmonious human interactions, it has a greater goal than harmony, for it relates not only to how we see and treat other humans, but to how we see and treat everything. Respect means taking time to see what is in front of us as fully and truthfully as possible so that we can make the sort of evaluative judgments that civility does not require.

For me—and I write as a Christian who claims to follow Jesus—respect is a disciplined set of attitudes and actions rooted in a way of seeing the world that reflects how God sees and acts in the world with patient, noncoercive love to redeem and recreate it through Jesus. I find helpful the words of Richard Mouw, a gentle Calvinist convinced of God's holiness, power, and wrath, who nevertheless writes: "God is a sovereign ruler—but in Jesus Christ he made it clear that he is that rare kind of ruler who comes to his people in the form of a servant. God is holy—but his holiness is revealed in his love for us. God is all-powerful—but his supreme power is displayed in the weakness and vulnerability of the cross."[3] If, out of respect for us and our freedom, God in Christ uses power with restraint, then respect ought to mark how God's church thinks and acts; name how Christians see and act in the world; and name how congregations see and exercise their identity, purpose, and ministry.

However, both the decline of the church in the West over recent decades and the fact that North American congregations are increasingly shunted to the margins of society make me ask if respect within, for, and from congregations characterizes how they think and act. Those who study why the church in Canada has declined since the mid-1960s most often identify secularism as the root cause.[4] That may be so, but I suspect that our congregations are crippled by a less ideological foe called disrespect, by which I mean not just the hurtful things Christians sometimes say and

---

3. Mouw, *Uncommon Decency*, 35.

4. For an analysis of the recent numerical decline of Canada's mainline denominations, see Clarke and Macdonald, *Leaving Christianity*.

do to each other, but the disrespect involved when, whether by design or default, congregations do not actually attend to the purpose for which God calls them into being. As we shall see, the biblical story of God's unfolding mission in the world considers local congregations as strategically vital, but I am not convinced that the leaders and members of most congregations think of their role in such elevated fashion.

Before proceeding, I will distinguish between respect and respectability; though they share the same etymological root, respect and respectability are not the same. To respect is to regard others and other things with great care. Respectability, on the other hand, is an ambiguous word. It may name the social acceptability that those with a reputation for integrity acquire, that may smooth their journey through life, thus making respectability a social good. On the other hand, the word "respectability" may name the approval that social-climbing people seek in an effort to distance themselves from those they deem less respectable. If respect exhibits itself in a caring attitude toward others, respectability may exhibit itself in shallow, dismissive judgments of others. At times, I suspect, congregations have sought (and still seek) the kind of respectability understood as society's approval more than they have respected others or even their own God-given identity.

As noted earlier, I became increasingly conscious of respect in church life while using the marriage liturgy in the Presbyterian Church in Canada's *Book of Common Worship*. It includes these words: "The apostles instructed those who enter into the marriage relationship to develop a mutual respect and love," and a prayer that the newlyweds will allow mutual respect to "nurture their individuality."[5] At first, mutual respect seemed to me to be too calculated to be linked with marital bliss, but the more I reflected, the more I appreciated the use of the word "respect" prior to the word "love"; after all, love covers a lot of territory and may refer to how we feel about our spouse or our SUV, to spiritual longing, or to sexual lust. What I discovered is that the couples with whom I met to plan marriage services often voiced appreciation for the fact that the phrase "mutual respect" gave moral clarity to the love they would pledge on their wedding day.

The word "respect" is now ubiquitous. After stating that all humans are "born free and equal in dignity and rights are endowed with reason and conscience and should act toward one another in a spirit of brotherhood," the preamble of the Universal Declaration of Human Rights (adopted by the United Nations General Assembly in 1948) promises that member

---

5. Presbyterian Church in Canada, *Book of Common Worship*, 170 and 177.

states will promote "universal respect" for those rights.[6] The era of respect had arrived, such that the word now appears in the mission statement of every hospital, school, and congregation. On the day I wrote this paragraph, the word "respect" appeared in two headlines of the daily newspaper I read. Its frequent use may suggest that it is now widely practiced or may reflect its absence. Environmentalists, for example, and those who protest abortion or the death penalty, all feel that they confront societies that lack respect for life; the sense that respect is lacking outrages current racial, religious, and sexual minorities. So, despite the United Nations General Assembly's view that "all human beings" are "born free and equal in dignity and rights," it seems respect is something for which many must fight.

Respect is a topic that has been discussed since ancient times. Aristotle (384–22 BCE) considered it a preeminent value and proposed the then-radical idea that it should be given not just for heroic action or military prowess but for moral worth. That sounds enlightened, yet it did not occur to Aristotle that slaves or those of limited intellectual ability might be among those to whom respect was due. For a very long time, respect remained exclusionary. Describing the Greco-Roman world in which Christianity first took root, Mark Finney says that the then–sought-after sources of honor or respect included noble birth, civic status, the social position of family and friends, wealth, the size of one's home and household, and one's moral reputation.[7] In addition, respect in ancient times was thought of as a limited good, such that to gain it meant that someone else had to lose it. Respect wasn't then considered an intrinsic value that belonged to every human being, but as something due to those whose achievement merited it or as something owed to those with status and power.

Finally, Immanuel Kant, the eighteenth-century German philosopher, challenged elitist definitions of respect. He built his ethics on the then-radical idea that respect is owed to every rational human being. All should be respected irrespective of moral worth for each "man and every reasonable agent exists as an end in himself," he argued.[8] For Kant, approval of gifted people or awe of powerful people was too arbitrary a basis on which to build respect. The son of a Lutheran pastor, he linked respect to the Bible's

---

6. Henkin, *International Bill of Rights*, 371–72.
7. Finney, *Honour and Conflict*, 37.
8. Kant, *Metaphysics of Ethics*, 39.

command to love our neighbor and the sense of rightness that follows when we "perform willingly all duties toward [our neighbor]."⁹

Before turning to respect for congregations, I want to acknowledge that my comments on respect in the paragraphs above and, indeed, my understanding of respect throughout the rest of this book, are derived from the lengthy and learned essay on respect in the *Stanford Encyclopedia of Philosophy*, written by Professor Robin Dillon in 2003 and since updated. Dillon's understanding of respect is compelling:

> First, as its derivation from the Latin *respicere*, (to look back at, look again) suggests, respect is a form of regard: a mode of attention to and acknowledgment of an object as something to be taken seriously. Respecting something contrasts with being oblivious or indifferent to it, ignoring or quickly dismissing it, neglecting or disregarding it, or carelessly or intentionally misidentifying it.
>
> We respect something not because we want to but because we recognize that we have to respect it . . . . In this way respect differs from, for example, liking and fearing, which have their sources in the subject's interests or desires. When we respect something, we heed its call, accord it its due, acknowledge its claim. Thus, respect involves deference, in the most basic sense of yielding to the object's demands.
>
> Other forms of respect are modes of valuing, appreciating the object as having worth or importance that is independent of, perhaps even at variance with, our desires or commitments. Thus, we can respect things we don't like or agree with, such as our enemies or someone else's opinion. Valuing respect is kin to esteem, admiration, veneration, reverence, and honor, while regarding something as utterly worthless or insignificant or disdaining or having contempt for it is incompatible with respecting it.¹⁰

To respect something, then, is to give it such careful attention that we see it, understand it, and appreciate it as it is in itself independent of our own interests, commitments, or desires. As I apply Dillon's definition of respect to congregations, I encourage congregational leaders to pay heed to what a congregation truly is, not "ignoring or quickly dismissing it, neglecting or disregarding it, or carelessly or intentionally misidentifying it," but grasping how the New Testament articulates the essence of a congregation's identity, the specificity of a congregation's purpose, and the pattern of a congregation's ministry.

9. Kant, *Metaphysics of Ethics*, 116.
10. Dillon, "Respect," §1.1.

Preliminary Musings on Respect

I suspect, however, that congregations often ignore their own identity and purpose. Until recently, North America's congregations, prominent in the life and landscape of every community, tended to take their existence and purpose for granted, and more than a few seem now to have no other obvious purpose than to serve as religious clubs for religious seniors. Aware of this, congregational leaders sometimes choose a new ministry to give their congregation a reason for being—maybe a new evangelism strategy, a new youth ministry, or a new anti-poverty initiative. But what sometimes happens is that congregational leaders try to fix their congregation's drift by imposing an identity on the congregation that is alien to its nature. A better approach is for a congregation to research and respect the theological identity, missional purpose, and ministry pattern offered to congregations by the New Testament, which I address in the chapters that follow.

If I rightly understand Dillon's essay, three types of respect dominate philosophical debate. The most traditional is what philosophers call *positional* respect; it honors those who occupy high positions even if they do not personally merit respect. Philosophers also talk of *appraisal* respect, given to those people and things evaluated as being worthy. It may be useful at this point to note that the appraised position of clergy in Canadian society has declined in status, such that respect is likely to be given only if clergy character and competence merit it. A third type of respect is Kant's view that all rational human beings ought to be respected, since all have inherent objective value, whether they are useful to us or not. But is respect an issue that ought to concern Christian congregations? Christians consider respect a "good thing," but it is hardly a topic on a theological par with the doctrine of the Trinity or the traditional claims that Christians make about Jesus, summarized in the Apostles' Creed. Nevertheless, I am convinced that a lack of respect *within*, and especially a lack of respect *for* congregations, severely hinders their effectiveness as communities called to witness to Jesus. In fact, I believe that respect, far from being an abstract philosophical idea, names the attitudes and actions that make—or fail to make—congregations what they ought to be.

RESPECTING CONGREGATIONS

Before looking at the theme of respect in relation to congregations, I first ask how respect has fared in the church at large. Generation after generation, the church has no doubt given respect to many; nevertheless, the church's failure to act with respect has frequently been spectacular. Emerging from an obscure province within the Roman Empire that suspected it, the church tried to convince that empire that it deserved, if not respect, at least tolerance. Aware of the vulnerability of the church, early Christian apologists presented the church, to those who suspected it, as a body of respectful believers who were also good citizens. Typical is the second-century *Apology of Aristides*, addressed to Hadrian, the Roman emperor:

> Now the Christians, O king . . . they commit neither adultery nor fornication; nor do they bear false witness, they do not deny a deposit, nor covet other men's goods: they honor father and mother and love their neighbors . . . . They do not do unto others that which they would not have done unto themselves. They comfort such as that wrong them and make friends of them: they labor to do good to their enemies.[11]

Centuries later, enjoying unimagined social status following the AD 312 conversion of the Emperor Constantine, the church within the Roman Empire no longer had to beg for respect. Rather, privileged and protected by that empire, the church refused to respect non-Christians. The early fifth-century Theodosian Code that set out a constitution for the recently Christianized Roman Empire decreed that non-Christian "pagans shall not be admitted to the imperial service, and they shall not be honored with the rank of administrator or judge," adding that though law-abiding Jews ought to be left in peace, the goods of Christian heretics were to be seized.[12]

Toleration for Jews did not last as, over the course of the succeeding millennium, church and state in medieval Europe built the social, legal, and political culture we know as Christendom. That culture practiced contempt for Jews and on occasion accompanied it with persecution. The advent of Protestantism in the sixteenth century did little to diminish this; at one point, Martin Luther called for Jewish homes and synagogues to be burned down.[13] This leads me to assert that, in its long history, the church has found it hard to act with respect when it has enjoyed power. It is only as the Western church's power and privilege diminished, following the Second World War, that respect could be said to mark Christian attitudes toward other religions.

---

11. Stevenson, *New Eusebius*, 56.
12. Stevenson, *Creeds, Councils, and Controversies*, 263.
13. Bainton, *Here I Stand*, 297.

Preliminary Musings on Respect

Respect, of course, does not mean we will always agree with others, nor does it mean that we will approve everything that claims our attention. Respect means that we will take seriously who others are and what they have to say. However, the cultural hegemony long enjoyed by the Western church encouraged a disrespect for non-Christian and non-Western people. While the modern missionary movement offers a record of sacrificial service given by Christians who greatly respected those whom they served, that record is marred by racist bigotry. Of Robert Moffat, an eminent Victorian missionary on whom the University of Edinburgh conferred an honorary doctor of divinity degree in 1872, Stephen Neill says, "In spite of his love for the Africans, he had little interest in the background of their thought and left behind no treasure of anthropological observation. He underestimated their religious traditions and introduced unaltered the fervent evangelical Christianity of his own tradition, without considering the possibilities of its adaptation to an African world. His methods were always and increasingly patriarchal."[14] A similar disrespect, I ought to add, was evident for a long time in the attitudes and actions of Canada's churches toward Canada's Indigenous Peoples.

In view of the Western church's frequent failure to respect non-Western and non-Christian people, what is required is humility. This is a challenge, not least for Christians who take seriously Jesus's command to go and make disciples of every nation. While that endeavor seeks to respect Christ's claim to be the Lord and Savior of the world, what often happens is that some mission-minded Christians eagerly proclaim but are slow to listen. Proclaiming Jesus is commendable, suggests John Stott, the influential evangelical leader, but not the lack of humility that prevents Christians from taking time to ask whether their speech and actions are respectful.[15]

The challenge of humility, along with the reluctance of zealous Christians to critique their speech and actions, also applies to congregations. As to how to treat others with respect, Richard Mouw offers the term "Christian civility," which, as noted earlier, overlaps with the meaning of respect. Being civil, says Mouw, does not commit Christians "to a *relativistic* perspective," does not mean "that we cannot criticize what goes on around us," and does not "require us to *approve* of what other people believe and do."[16] Though what Mouw has in mind is how Christians relate to those of

---

14. Neill, *History of Christian Missions*, 313.
15. See Stott, *Christian Mission*, 72–81.
16. Mouw, *Uncommon Decency*, 22. Italics original.

other faiths or none, his words also apply to attitudes and actions *within* congregations, where respect calls for an openness to learning about and from others, each of whom has value before God.

Of course, a common expectation is that congregational members will respect one another, but that does not always happen. Think, for example, of ego-driven clergy who refuse to apologize, or who pay only lip service to seeking God's vision for congregations. Or think of how congregational worship is hijacked to serve purposes other than an encounter between God and God's people. During my years teaching theological students, I visited many congregations. In some, respect was palpable in the welcome given to newcomers, in the integrity of clergy, and in the compassion that congregational members displayed; in others, disrespect appeared in sloppy liturgical leadership and in how congregational members talked to and about one another. Disrespect *within* congregations, in whatever form it appears, leads to muddled ministry and hurt believers.

Consider the following: During one congregation's Sunday worship, the minister suspended the service so that the congregation could listen to a radio broadcast of a hockey game, hockey being Canada's national religion! That disrespect still shocks me. In another congregation, during a meeting of its session (the term in Presbyterian polity for the elected leaders of a congregation), the minister—whose role it is to chair such meetings—was asked to leave so that the others could discuss whether to grant her study leave. That session's disrespect was twofold: first, a session cannot meet unless a minister is there to chair it; second, that session would know that an annual study leave is guaranteed within a minister's call, not something granted at the pleasure of a session. In this example, a group of mostly older men treated a young, female, visible minority minister with disrespect.

Beyond examples of disrespect *within* congregations, the chapters that follow address the lack of respect *for* congregations, displayed when they fail to grasp, embody, and exhibit what God calls them to be and to do. To illustrate what I mean, I recall attending a Fuller Institute Church Growth conference in the late 1980s, where I learned to think of congregational leadership not just as a list of discrete pastoral tasks to be done, but as the capacity to see the congregation as a complex system. I found and still find this insight to be very helpful, yet I also recall that one speaker at the conference advised us that, seeking church growth and effective time management, we should divide our congregational members into four categories:

Preliminary Musings on Respect

VIPs, or very important people; VTPs, very teachable people; VNPs, very nice people; and VDPs, very draining people.

As I and others mentally placed various members of our congregations back home into each category, the speaker made the point that investing time and energy on VNPs and VDPs is an anti-growth strategy! This struck me as disrespectful of what a congregation is. What would Jesus make of it, given that the Gospels report how he allowed himself to be endlessly interrupted by needy people—a colony of people suffering from leprosy, a woman with a twelve-year hemorrhage, a widow grieving her son, and various "sinners" whom others habitually and publicly shamed? While a "systems" approach to congregations can be helpful, no system ought to encourage their leaders to disrespect anyone, whether important, teachable, nice, or draining, or to impose on a congregation an identity so alien to its true nature.

By way of contrast, consider the respect with which the apostle Paul describes Corinth's congregation in 1 Cor 3:26–31:

> Not many of you were wise by human standards, not many were powerful, not many were of noble birth. But God chose what is foolish in the world to shame the wise; God chose what is weak in the world to shame the strong; God chose what is low and despised in the world, things that are not, to reduce to nothing things that are, so that no one might boast in the presence of God. He is the source of your life in Christ Jesus, who became for us wisdom from God, and righteousness and sanctification and redemption.

Implicit in this text is a quite different understanding of what the identity of a congregation is as compared with a VIP, VTP, VNP, VDP church growth strategy. Yes, congregations act like other organizations in some ways, and may usefully adopt and adapt organizational systems, skills, and strategies. But congregations, called into being by the God whom Jesus revealed, have a unique DNA that often leads them to contradict how organizations typically operate. That must be respected!

To conclude, I am convinced that respect *within* and especially *for* congregations will help them to give winsome Christian witness. But more important is my conviction that respect is a thoroughly biblical concern. The whole New Testament, written to edify and equip congregations that are called to witness to Jesus, ought to be read as a collection of congregational documents that conveys a remarkable respect for what congregations are and what God calls them to do. This point, while not familiar to most congregations, is well made by the missional theologian Darrell Guder: "The congregations founded by the first missionaries had, as their purpose, the continuation of the witness that had led to their founding. The writings that became the canonic New Testament all functioned basically as instruments for the continuing formation of these communities for the faithful fulfillment of their missional vocation."[17] So, I turn now to the Bible, and particularly to the New Testament, to explore how respect shows up and to trace in greater detail its respect *for* congregations.

---

17. Guder, *Called to Witness*, 13.

2

The Bible's Respect for Congregations

LIKE MOST CHRISTIANS, I consider the Bible foundational for Christians. So, I am curious about what the Bible says about respect and, in particular, what the New Testament says about the identity, purpose, and ministry of Christian congregations. But while individual believers are urged to read the Bible in search of food for their souls, and church denominations invariably search the Bible to find a base for their creedal claims, I am not sure that congregations are expected to go to the Bible to locate their place and purpose in its unfolding story of God's work in the world. However, in this chapter and those that follow, I will try to do that, though I am not a professional biblical scholar, and though the word "respect" is disconcertingly rare in English-language bibles.

RESPECT IN THE BIBLE

I have never read a book that addresses the idea of respect in the Bible. The word seldom appears within it; if infrequent in the King James Version (KJV), it is even less so in the New Revised Standard Version (NRSV). For example, Gen 4:4–5 in the KJV is "The Lord had respect unto Abel and to his offering. But unto Cain and to his offering he had not respect," while the NRSV has "The Lord had regard for Abel and his offering, but for Cain and his offering he had no regard." Deuteronomy 1:17 in the KJV reads "Ye shall not respect persons in judgment; but ye shall hear the small as well as the great," while the NRSV has "You must not be partial in judging; hear out the small and the great alike." Isaiah 17:7 in the KJV has "At that day shall a man look to his Maker, and his eyes shall have respect to the Holy One of Israel," while the NRSV has "On that day people will regard their Maker, and their eyes will look to the Holy One of Israel."

As illustrated above, English translations of the Bible use alternative words and phrases for respect, such as awe, give regard to, pay attention to, revere, or honor, words that translate Hebrew words in the Old Testament that echo the types of respect I named in chapter 1. The call in Deut 1:17 for Israel to respect "the small and the great" echoes Kant's view that all humans are to be respected; in Isa 17:7, the call for Israel to "look to the Holy One of Israel" approximates to the *positional* respect most societies give to divine and human leaders; and the Gen 4 story of God evaluating Abel's and Cain's offerings so differently approximates to *appraisal* respect. If not often explicit, respect appears in the Bible as an implicit set of attitudes and actions expected of God's people.

Positional respect, which the Old Testament prominently gives to God as the source of all power and worth, means honoring God. It finds classic expression in the First Commandment: "I am the Lord your God . . . you shall have no other gods before me" (Exod 20:2). But the Bible seeks to elicit for God, the Holy One of Israel, an appraised as well as a positional respect. Psalm 96 is an example: "O sing to the Lord a new song; sing to the Lord, all the earth. Sing to the Lord, bless his name; tell of his salvation from day to day. Declare his glory among the nations . . . . For great is the Lord, and greatly to be praised; he is to be revered above all gods." As to why Ps 96 and so many others command that God be praised and receive ultimate respect, C. S. Lewis states that the command does not spring from God's ego but from the conviction that God is so glorious that our praise "is the correct, adequate or appropriate response . . . and if we do not admire we shall be stupid, insensible, and great losers."[1] Indeed, 1 Sam 2:12 calls the sons of Eli the priest "scoundrels" who "had no regard for the Lord or for the duties of the priests," a disregard that led to the fall of the priestly house of Eli (1 Sam 2:30).

The oft-repeated Old Testament command that God be honored and worshiped is strikingly expanded in the New Testament to include Jesus. His earliest followers were not only attracted to Jesus but confessed him to

---

1. Lewis, *Reflections on the Psalms*, 78.

be and worshiped him as God. This identity is explicitly promoted in the Gospel of John, which reports Jesus saying that God the Father and God the Son work in unity "so that all may honor the Son just as they honor the Father" (5:23). Though less explicit, the Synoptic Gospels make similar claims about Jesus. Take, for example, Matt 28:16–20a:

> Now the eleven disciples went to Galilee, to the mountain to which Jesus had directed them. When they saw him, they worshipped him; but some doubted. And Jesus came and said to them, "All authority in heaven and on earth has been given to me. Go therefore and make disciples of all nations, baptizing them in the name of the Father and of the Son and of the Holy Spirit, and teaching them to obey everything that I have commanded you."

Jesus's claim to have "all authority" over "all nations" runs as a thread through the New Testament. It appears, for example, in Eph 1:20–22, where the apostle Paul wrote that God raised Jesus "from the dead and seated him at his right hand in the heavenly places, far above all rule and authority and power and dominion, and above every name that is named . . . and he has put all things under his feet and has made him the head over all things." The belief that Jesus was raised from the dead, crucial to the formation of Christian congregations, led Paul in 1 Cor 8:6 to join the honoring of the Son to that of the Father by writing or quoting the following Christian expansion of the Jewish Shema (Deut 6:4): "There is one God, the Father, from whom all things exist, and one Lord, Jesus Christ, through whom are all things and through whom we exist." This text, says Richard Hays, does not directly address Jesus's divine status, yet "verse 6 takes the extraordinarily bold step of identifying 'the Lord Jesus' with 'the Lord' acclaimed in the *Shema*, while still insisting that 'for us there is one God.' Paul and other early Christians," says Hays, "reshaped Israel's faith in such a way that Jesus is now acclaimed as Lord within the framework of monotheism."[2]

I emphasize Jesus's status in the New Testament because belief in his elevated status gave birth to and shaped the identity of the first Christian congregations. To illustrate, the word *kurios* (meaning "Lord"), which is used in the Greek Old Testament to render the Hebrew word *Adonai* (a circumlocution for God's sacred name), is applied in the New Testament to Jesus. According to Oscar Cullmann, this reveals that "early Christianity does not hesitate to transfer to Jesus everything the Old Testament says

---

2. Hays, *First Corinthians*, 140.

about God."³ This is astonishing, as is the fact that Jesus's first disciples, all of them monotheistic Jews, accepted the exalted status of Jesus once convinced that he had risen from the dead. Their readiness to so recognize Jesus led them to obey his famous command to go and make disciples, who, of course, were then formed into congregations.

As to the apostle Paul, another monotheistic Jew, he confessed Jesus as Lord, referring to him in the 1 Cor 16:22 phrase, "Our Lord, come." In that phrase, however, Paul does not use the Greek word *kurios* but the Aramaic word *maranatha*—Aramaic being the language spoken by Palestinian Jews in Jesus's day. The New Testament scholar F. F. Bruce sees this Aramaic word as testifying "to the place given to the exalted and expected Christ in the worship of the most primitive church."[4] Early Christianity and its earliest congregations located in Palestine thus gave a supreme place to Jesus. This high honoring of Jesus was central to the identity of New Testament congregations, such that his name became "the name that is above every name" (Phil 2:9), the name confessed by Christians at their baptism (Rom 10:9), and the only name "under heaven given among mortals by which we must be saved" (Acts 4:12).

That early congregations named Jesus as Lord in a pluralist society with many "lords" led to their being suspect and even persecuted. North American congregations, also now living in a pluralist culture that suspects those who make exclusive religious claims, are tempted to use the generic word "God" rather than risk the scandal of particularity that naming Jesus involves. But if it is true that confessing Jesus as Lord defined congregations in New Testament times, that fundamental fact about Christian congregations must be fully respected by Christian congregations now. But is it? I will return to this issue after I complete a brief survey of respect in the Bible.

The Bible's command that God be honored extends to things and people associated with God. Accordingly, Lev 22:2 (NIV) commands that the priests of Israel "treat with respect the sacred offerings the Israelites consecrate" to God, with verse 9 warning those priests not to treat their priestly service "with contempt." As to people associated with God who are to be honored, the Bible includes parents in a position of authority over children, and kings and civil authorities in positions of authority over us. The apostle Paul reflects this positional respect in his command that "every person be subject to the governing authorities," adding that we are to "pay . . . what

---

3. Cullmann, *Christology of the New Testament*, 307.
4. Bruce, *1 and 2 Corinthians*, 162.

The Bible's Respect for Congregations

is due them . . . respect to whom respect is due," since the authorities are "God's servants" (Rom 13:6). On occasion, the Bible gives appraisal respect to some who did not occupy an exalted position—Mordecai (Esth 8:15), Joseph (Matt 1:19), Mary (Luke 1:30), or Barnabas (Acts 11:19–20). Then there is Solomon, who enjoyed positional respect as Israel's king but also received God's appraised respect for choosing, as a gift from God, not more honor or glory for himself but the wisdom to rule. God's comment is this: "I give you also what you have not asked, both riches and honor all your life" (1 Kgs 3:13).

Besides positional and appraisal respect, the Bible commands a broad respect for others, which includes widows, orphans, and the poor. Deuteronomy 1:17, for example, warns Israel's leaders not to be "partial in judging" but to "hear out the small and the great alike." In the book of Ruth, Boaz shows this respect to his needy, widowed relative Naomi and her foreign-born daughter-in-law Ruth. God's desire that the poor be respected reappears in the New Testament, in Jas 2:2–6, for example, as a quality to be practiced in congregational life: "If a person with gold rings and in fine clothes comes into your assembly, and if a poor person in dirty clothes also comes in, and if you take notice of the one wearing the fine clothes and say, 'Have a seat here, please,' while to the one who is poor you say, 'Stand there,' or 'Sit at my feet,' have you not made distinctions among yourselves . . . you have dishonored the poor."

For James and for the Bible generally, respect for the poor is rooted in the character of God, who gives "to all generously and ungrudgingly" (Jas 1:5); as Ps 138:6 says, "Though the Lord is high, he regards the lowly," or as 1 Sam 2:7–8 reports Hannah saying, "The Lord makes poor and makes rich; he brings low, he also exalts. He raises up the poor from the dust; he lifts the needy from the ash heap, to make them sit with princes and inherit a seat of honor."

That said, the Bible does not present respect as a set of universal rights, though Ps 8 hints in that direction. Awed by creation's beauty, the psalmist asks why a sovereign God is "mindful of" mortals, and answers that God made humans "a little lower than God and crowned them with glory and honor," giving them "dominion over the works of your hands." Reading Ps 8 as an echo of Gen 1, James L. Mays comments, "Being human means being ordained and installed in a right and responsibility within the divine sovereignty";[5] that is, God's respect for us lies in our God-given vocation as

---

5. Mays, *Psalms*, 69.

caretakers of God's world, not in any innate human capacity. Though Mays notes that we fail to fulfill the office God has assigned, Ps 8 maintains the respected position for humans. Likewise, Richard Mouw, reflecting on Gen 1, writes that "God created all human beings. Even the shattered and broken ones are still his original works of art. We must engage in the spiritual exercise of seeing others as God sees them, of appreciating others—even in their brokenness."[6] Commenting on this biblical climate of respect, Mouw writes, "God wants us to offer a fundamental respect to others purely on the basis of their humanness. Christians and Muslims, African Americans and Jewish Americans, heterosexuals and homosexuals, rich and poor—all are created in the divine likeness."[7]

Moving on to how congregations ought to act with respect, 1 Peter articulates a set of attitudes and actions expected of Christian congregations in response to their being insulted and shamed by the dominant culture of that day. First Peter 2:4 notes that some whom God honors will be despised by the world, as was Jesus, and adds that like Jesus, his followers, if despised, remain in God's eyes "a chosen race, a royal priesthood, a holy nation, God's own people" (1 Pet 2:9). Like Jesus, God's people are not to return abuse or treat others with contempt, but are to live "honorably among the Gentiles, so that . . . they may see your honorable deeds and glorify God" (1 Pet 2:12), and even "accept the authority of every human institution, whether of the emperor or of governors, as sent by him to punish those who do wrong" (1 Pet 2:13). This verse seems to expect unqualified respect for civil authorities, but Joel Green notes that the respect Peter asked believers to give is qualified by the fact that it is to be given "for the Lord's sake" (1 Pet 2:13) by "servants of God [who] live as free people" (1 Pet 2:16). He further argues that the call for believers to be respectful—"Honor everyone. Love the family of believers, Fear God. Honor the emperor" (1 Pet 2:17)—far from implying approval of the status quo, is deeply subversive. Commenting on the words "Honor everyone . . . Honor the emperor," Green writes, "It is hard to imagine a more devastating critique of the Roman way, for with the pairing of these two directives, Peter has flattened the status pyramid of the Roman world. He has just made one's response to the slave next door no less than one's response to the emperor."[8]

---

6. Mouw, *Uncommon Decency*, 73–74.
7. Mouw, *Uncommon Decency*, 40.
8. Green, *1 Peter*, 76.

The Bible's Respect for Congregations

That Christians should act respectfully if insulted is unsurprising, given that the Gospels portray Jesus's respect for those treated with contempt. Luke 15:2, for example, reports how Jesus taught, forgave, and invited "sinners" to be his disciples, while the Pharisees "grumbled" against them. Typical is the Mark 9 account of Jesus placing a little child (then assumed to be a low-status being) among his disciples, who were arguing about which of them was the greatest, and then telling them, "Whoever welcomes one such child in my name welcomes me" (Mark 9:36–37). Then there is the Mark 5:21–34 story of Jesus's respect for Jairus, a synagogue leader who begged him to heal his sick daughter, and Jesus's equal respect for a nameless woman who, having "suffered from hemorrhages for twelve years," hoped to be healed anonymously by touching Jesus's cloak. She was healed, but not anonymously. Bernie Skelding, minister at St. Andrew's Church, Niagara-on-the-Lake, which I attend, gave me permission to quote from his sermon on this story:

> She had taken his power, but Jesus wanted to give her something better.... With one word Jesus gave this nameless lonely woman, a new name, and a new relationship... Jesus called her daughter; in that one word was more power than she had taken; in that one word, that one name, Jesus welcomed her into a profound relationship with himself—a Daughter of the living God.... I wonder when she last heard someone call her daughter. Or wanted to be that close to her? I wonder when she last heard someone speak to her with such gentleness, such kindness, such inclusion, treat her with such respect with so much dignity... Daughter—as if to say... Daughter—I see you, I know you, you are not alone. Daughter—you have riches beyond imagination. Daughter—your body is healed, your soul is restored, you are loved with a love no less than the love that Jairus has for his daughter. Even more than Jairus longs for his daughter's healing, so I long for yours.[9]

The word "respect" never appears in the Gospels, yet Jesus's respect shines from every page, suggesting that respect should mark how his disciples respond to both God and those made in God's image. As Dillon's essay in the *Stanford Encyclopedia of Philosophy* says, respect does not imply approval of what others think or do; it means refusing to dismiss others with contempt.

---

9. St. Andrew's Presbyterian Church, "Thanksgiving Sunday."

THE NEW TESTAMENT'S RESPECT FOR CONGREGATIONS

To begin, I pay attention to the New Testament Greek word *ekklesia*, which appears sixty times in the apostle Paul's letters and is most prominent in 1 Corinthians. Paul wrote 1 Corinthians after learning about problems in the congregation he had begun in Corinth, one of which was that some congregational members were treating other members with contempt.

Mark Finney writes that, in Paul's day, Roman citizens "lusted after honor and were determined to be seen, and publicly acknowledged, as having the social rewards which honor brought—status, respect, power, influence."[10] Angry that lust for honor had infiltrated Corinth's congregation and had divided it into factions, its founder Paul reminded it that, according to Greco-Roman values, he lacked honor as a homeless manual worker and former prisoner (1 Cor 4:9–13), and later added, "we proclaim Jesus Christ as Lord and ourselves as your slaves" (2 Cor 4:5). As everyone knew, slaves were due no respect whatever! As to factions in the congregation, one seems to have considered itself socially superior and free to treat other congregants with contempt; another faction seems to have considered itself a spiritually elite group because of its ability to speak in tongues; yet another seems to have thought itself an intellectually wise elite.

Unsurprisingly, Paul addresses the issue of congregational identity, implicitly touching on congregational conflict in the opening words of 1 Corinthians by naming the congregation "the church [*ekklesia*] of God that is in Corinth . . . those who are sanctified in Christ Jesus, called to be saints" (1 Cor 1:2). *Ekklesia* was a widely used word in Greek society that named a local assembly of citizens meeting for political or civic reasons. Paul would also have read the word *ekklesia* in the Greek Old Testament, where it translates the Hebrew words *qahal* and *eda* that refer to Israel when its citizens gathered before God in part or in whole. Whether applied to gathered Jews or gathered Christians, *ekklesia* referred to an assembly of people called together to meet God. Paul's frequent use of the word points to his conviction that the gospel appropriated by individual believers has major social and communal implications.

To reinforce what it meant for Corinth's congregation to be an *ekklesia*, Paul uses three metaphors in 1 Cor 3:9–16 that identify it as God's field, building, and temple, clarifying that an *ekklesia* is a community that God plants, constructs, and inhabits—even Corinth's *ekklesia*, marked by

---

10. Finney, *Honour and Conflict*, 35.

significant division. For Paul, a congregation belongs to God; it is God's work before it is that of local leaders, even though God may use the latter as field hands!

But before further articulating what Paul says about congregational identity, I suggest that the significance of Paul calling a congregation an *ekklesia* is obscured when English translations of the New Testament translate the word as "church" rather than "congregation." "Church" is not wrong, but "congregation" better translates *ekklesia* in most New Testament texts; as *The Oxford Companion to the Bible* notes, Paul used *ekklesia* "in his letters to address individual communities of believers... Paul does not have a developed sense of the church as a universal institution but rather sees local assemblies of believers functioning independently in separate locations."[11]

Aware that *ekklesia* in the New Testament most often refers to a local assembly, William Tyndale, an early convert to Lutheranism, translated *ekklesia* as "congregation" in his 1526 English New Testament and faced a political and ecclesiastical storm for doing so, as had Luther when he translated *ekklesia* as *gemeinde* ("congregation") not *kirche* ("church") in his 1522 German New Testament. Tyndale and Luther preferred "congregation" to "church" because it reflects what the New Testament usually means by *ekklesia*, a local assembly; whereas the word "church" had, over the centuries, assumed institutional and global associations, and for sixteenth-century Reformers like Luther and Tyndale carried with it unwelcome Roman Catholic associations. In translating *ekklesia* as "congregation," they followed Erasmus, then Europe's best Greek scholar; however, Calvin did not. He comments on the phrase "With the church that is in their household," found in 1 Cor 16:19: "The word 'congregation,' which Erasmus preferred, is not in line with what Paul had in mind. For he did not mean to describe a mere crowd of people, and use an ordinary word to do so, but to speak with great respect about the organization of a particular Christian household."[12]

The translation of *ekklesia* as congregation in English bibles did not long survive Tyndale. When King James VI of Scotland succeeded Queen Elizabeth I of England in 1603, Puritans in the Church of England urged him to call a conference, hoping that James, raised as a Presbyterian, might grant a deeper reform of the English Church than Elizabeth. The subsequent 1604 Hampton Court Conference quashed those hopes but did approve a new translation of the Bible. With that approval, however, came

---

11. Schowalter, "Church," 122.
12. Calvin, *Calvin's Commentaries*, 356.

instructions from the archbishop of Canterbury to the Bible translation teams that they were to translate *ekklesia* as "church," not "congregation." The word "congregation" was then simply too anti-episcopal and anti-monarchist in its associations to appear in a Bible that sought the approval of the episcopal Church of England and its supreme governor the king.[13]

To this day, *ekklesia* is translated as "church" in almost all English-language bibles. This, I suggest, obscures for readers of Paul's letters his insights about the identity, purpose, and ministry of local congregations. I say that because, for many readers, the word "church" will be read, not as referring to a local congregation, but to the less local, less concrete entity that the Apostles' Creed calls "the holy catholic Church." Of course, *ekklesia* is rightly translated as "church" in texts such as Eph 1:22 and Col 1:18, where what is in view is not a local assembly but the church as a broad corporate entity. But even in these verses, argues Robert Banks, what Paul refers to as "church" is not what we now think of as the worldwide church, an idea foreign to Paul, but to the church that lives in the heavenly realm. Christians, writes Banks, "belong both to a heavenly church which is permanently in session and to a local church, which . . . is a tangible expression of the heavenly church."[14]

Translating *ekklesia* as "church" rather than "congregation," by obscuring Paul's interest in local, visible congregations, makes it hard for today's congregations to see themselves reflected in the New Testament, and discourages them from going to the New Testament to discover their place and purpose in God's mission. But congregational identity is also obscured in another way in English-language bibles. In the KJV, "thou" is used for the single pronoun "you" and "ye" is used for the plural pronoun "you"; but that distinction disappears in current English bibles that consistently use "you" as both a single and plural pronoun. Take the 1 Cor 3:23 phrase "you belong to Christ," for example; though Paul occasionally uses "you" as a single pronoun to refer to individuals—in 1 Cor 6 he tells some individuals in Corinth's church not to consort with prostitutes—he most often uses "you" as a plural pronoun to refer to a congregation, as in 1 Cor 3:23, where his phrase "you belong to Christ" reminds a congregation fighting over various church leaders that it does not belong to any human leader but to Christ himself.

---

13. Nicholson, *God's Secretaries*, 75.
14. Banks, *Paul's Idea of Community*, 42.

The Bible's Respect for Congregations

It is, of course, legitimate to use the pronoun "you" in the Bible as a singular pronoun in some instances, but it is unfortunate when "you" is read individualistically when the New Testament intends for it to refer to congregations. Consider these texts: "Do you not know that you are God's temple and that God's Spirit dwells in you?" (1 Cor 3:16); "Keep alert, stand firm in your faith, be courageous, be strong. Let all that you do be done in love" (1 Cor 16:13); "You know the generous act of our Lord Jesus Christ, that though he was rich, yet for your sakes he became poor, so that by his poverty you might become rich" (2 Cor 8:9). Paul wrote these texts to tell Corinth's congregation that, loved by Jesus and indwelt by the Spirit, it was blessed and thus could bless others. But such texts, if read individualistically as they so often are, hide Paul's hope for how congregations should think and act. As Richard Hays says, Paul is not "concerned just with individual edification of believers or with doctrinal teaching in the abstract.... His constant goal is to call the Corinthians to understand their corporate existence as the church."[15] That goal is hindered both by the nonuse of "congregation" in English-language bibles and the habitual reading of "you" in those bibles as a singular pronoun when its reference is plural.

Before proceeding, I want to clarify that in emphasizing what the New Testament says to and about congregations, I do not seek in any way to diminish the Bible's emphasis on the faith and life of individuals. God's interest in and commitment to individuals, so prominent in the biblical narrative—think of Abram, Sarah, Moses, Naomi, Ruth, David, Esther, Jeremiah, Amos, Mary, Peter, John, Paul—remains to this day, as the Holy Spirit calls us to faith and sustains our personal faith. Yet it must be noted that the Bible consistently locates individual believers within a covenant community, the community that the New Testament addressed as it took on visible form as apostolic-era congregations.

Now to my original point: in the New Testament, a congregation is God's *ekklesia*. Yet current congregational literature rarely identifies congregations as God's *ekklesia* and instead thinks of and treats them as organizations that astute leaders can fix. But as John Leith says, "Nowhere in the New Testament is there the slightest indication that the church is a human organization that came into being according to human plans . . . there is always emphasis on the prior activity of God."[16] Leith is correct: Paul was adamant that a congregation is a God-created community. Nevertheless,

---

15. Hays, *First Corinthians*, 11.
16. Leith, *Basic Christian Doctrine*, 235.

Paul knew, and we know, that though a congregation is much more than a human organization, it is not less than one, which is why 1 Cor 1:2 refers to Corinth's congregation as a community that lives not only "in Christ" but that lives "in Corinth."

Think first about the "in Corinth" identity of Corinth's congregation. Once a prosperous Greek port that fell to the Romans in 146 BCE, Corinth lay abandoned for almost a century before Roman colonists resettled it. Two generations later, Paul began a church there, most of its members being gentile converts. The apostle then moved on, later writing to the congregation to remind it of its identity "in Christ." As to its local "in Corinth" identity, much of that can only now be surmised from odd references in 1 and 2 Corinthians and by reading between the lines. But this we know: whether in Corinth, Calgary, or Chicago, congregations inevitably adopt a local form and identity. In Canada, congregations are shaped by the fact that, to meet, a building is required, one that for many months of the year requires a source of heat and someone to turn it on! If hyper-spiritual believers think this a sign of retrograde spirituality, they fail to respect that a congregation, though more than, is never less than a social organization.

Corinth's congregation took local form as a group of house churches (1 Cor 16:15–19), who likely all assembled on "the first day of every week" (1 Cor 16:2). At such a gathering, Paul expected his letter (1 Corinthians) to be read to the congregation; in it, he instructs leaders to review Corinth's worship (1 Cor 11–14), deal with its difficult people (1 Cor 5:1–2), and organize a collection for the congregation in Jerusalem (1 Cor 16:2–3). Though God's *ekklesia* in Corinth had been initiated by an apostle, local leaders were clearly required to address ordinary, ongoing issues. Paul took it for granted that such local leaders were in place to address such issues—and also some extraordinary issues, for in 1 Cor 5, Paul calls them to discipline a sexually deviant congregational member.

Another aspect of the "in Corinth" identity of Corinth's congregation is revealed by its weak response to Paul's request that it help Jerusalem's struggling congregation (1 Cor 16:1). Writing later to Corinth's congregation, Paul contrasts its financial reluctance with the generosity of Macedonia's churches (2 Cor 8:1–7). Today's congregational leaders know about such issues and know, too, about congregational conflict. In his Corinthian letters, Paul confronts conflict head on, illustrated in the following verses: "Can it be that there is no one among you wise enough to decide between one believer and another?" (1 Cor 6:5); "The husband should give to his

The Bible's Respect for Congregations

wife her conjugal rights, and likewise the wife to her husband" (1 Cor 7:3); "When you come together . . . If anyone speaks in a tongue, let there be only two or at most three" (1 Cor 14:26–27). Meanwhile, in Phil 4:2, Paul urges a Philippian church leader to sort out a rift between two women, Euodia and Syntyche, and in 1 Thess 5:14 he tells the Thessalonian church leaders "to admonish idlers, encourage the fainthearted, help the weak [and] be patient with all of them."

Paul's approach to conflict in congregations is noteworthy. While current theories about congregational leadership focus on creating a vision and having others catch it, Paul's leadership seems to have been just as much a matter of doing what was required to sustain congregational life—facing conflict by both comforting and confronting congregants, being ready to make decisions that not everyone will approve of, using common sense as well as prayer to discern direction, and respecting the fact that congregational members are capable of being as difficult and devious as any other human beings.

What I have just written tries to tease out from 1 Corinthians a few clues as to the local identity of Corinth's congregation, an identity that is shaped by a congregation's history, decision-making processes, resources, personalities, size, and organizational form, all of which make each congregation unique. New Testament congregations, being recent, had a short history and few material resources—the era of looking after church buildings lay in the future—yet such congregations developed their own style as each faced unique circumstances as a community of unique individuals.

Beyond local identity, on which current congregational literature rightly focuses, New Testament congregations were shaped by their "in Christ" identity. To this issue I now turn. As noted earlier, the first Christian congregations were defined by what they made of Jesus. Though they differed significantly in ethnic makeup and location, those congregations shared a common identity "in Christ," an identity that the New Testament sees as key for any congregation in any generation, culture, or location. For a congregation to respect that identity, it must, as Robin Dillon puts it, "heed its call, accord it its due, acknowledge its claim."[17]

Accordingly, while Paul offered practical advice to local congregations, he regularly addressed a congregation's local issues by way of its "in Christ" identity. So, in 1 Corinthians, as he names the pressures on Corinth's congregation to conform to the city's social and sexual mores, eat meat offered to local idols, and engage in Corinth's contests for honor, Paul repeatedly

---

17. Dillon, "Respect," §1.1.

calls the congregation to respect its identity in Christ. "In the first ten verses of Paul's First Letter to the Corinthians," notes William Barclay, "the name of Jesus Christ occurs no fewer than ten times." Likewise, Paul's letter to the Philippians names Jesus Christ seven times in its first eleven verses. Barclay comments, "Sometimes in the Church we try to deal with a difficult situation by means of a book of laws or rules or regulations; sometimes we try to deal with it in the spirit of human justice; sometimes . . . we try to deal with a difficult situation in our own mental and spiritual power. Paul did none of those things; to his difficult situation he took Jesus."[18]

Paul's habit of tackling a congregation's local issues by referring to its "in Christ" identity is not now as common; yet to that identity I turn, again chiefly relying on 1 Corinthians. I begin with the known yet undeveloped fact that the New Testament identifies congregations as families. Paul evokes this by calling congregational members "brothers and sisters," "the family of faith," (Gal 6:10), and the "children of God" who are to call God "Abba! Father!" (Rom 8:14–16). Paul reinforces this familial identity by frequently using "one another" language in congregations—love one another, pray for one another, greet one another, bear with one another—and his hope that family-like congregations will exhibit such mutual care that "if one member suffers, all suffer together . . . if one member is honored, all rejoice together" (1 Cor 12:26). At the same time, Paul does not think of family-like congregations sentimentally. Take 1 Cor 13:4–8a: "Love is patient; love is kind; love is not envious or boastful or arrogant or rude. It does not insist on its own way; it is not irritable or resentful; it does not rejoice in wrongdoing but rejoices in the truth. It bears all things, believes all things, hopes all things, endures all things. Love never ends." In these verses, Paul indicates that he is well aware of how challenging the family life of a congregation can be.

To grasp how significant it is that the New Testament identifies a congregation as a family, consider the following family-related issues in the Gospels. First, the family genealogies found in the Old Testament disappear in the New. Second, when his mother, Mary, and brothers came to speak to Jesus, he asked, "Who is my mother, and who are my brothers?" Pointing to his disciples, he said, "Here are my mother and my brothers! For whoever does the will of my father in heaven is my brother and sister and mother" (Matt 12:46). Third, Matt 19 reports that Jesus's disciples, dismayed by his restrictive attitude to divorce, were shocked by his alternative—singleness.

---

18. Barclay, *Letters to the Corinthians*, 10.

The Bible's Respect for Congregations

Jews at the time took it for granted that all would marry, be fruitful, and multiply. But for Jesus, though marriage remained important, he relativized it, leaving him and others free to choose singleness as a legitimate option to marriage. Reflecting on these issues two decades ago, I wrote the following about how the New Testament redefines family:

> The people of God, since Jesus, is not constituted according to the flesh or by physical lineage and is not dependent on marriage and physical procreation. To be a child of God, in the New Testament, is to be born of the Spirit. Hence human genealogy no longer carries the same theological weight. But not only do the genealogical lists disappear; they are, I suggest, replaced by texts like Romans 16, where Paul provides a list of the women and men, the free and the slaves, the married and the single, who constitute his new family of brothers and sisters in Christ . . . . The church of the New Testament grows by witness to the stranger rather than through biology, and the nature of the family is changed as those who were once strangers enter the family of God and become brothers and sisters . . . . For Jesus, and for Paul, the kingdom of God, the new creation, has broken into history; the new age has begun. This is what comes first for all believers.[19]

Rodney Clapp's book *Families at the Crossroads* goes further to argue that the New Testament prioritizes the church as first family over the biological family: "The church is God's most important institution on earth. The church is the social agent that most significantly shapes and forms the character of Christians. And the church is the primary vehicle of God's grace and salvation for a waiting, desperate world."[20] I agree with Clapp, though I wish that in emphasizing the importance of character formation, he had noted that such formation is largely delivered by congregations, which are too often unnamed and hidden behind "the church."

The New Testament, then, considers a congregation as a family, but not one that lives a private life behind its front door. To the contrary, Paul told the congregation in Ephesus, "I . . . beg you to lead a life worthy of the calling to which you have been called . . . putting away falsehood, let all of us speak the truth to our neighbors" (Eph 4:1, 25). To the congregation in Colossae he wrote, "Conduct yourselves wisely toward outsiders . . . . Let your speech always be gracious, seasoned with salt" (Col 4:5). Those texts call congregations to live in neighborhoods as communities publicly marked by

---

19. Ervine, "Single in the Church," 221–22.
20. Clapp, *Families at the Crossroads*, 67.

such truth-telling, honest work, gracious speech, and kindness to the needy (Eph 4:25–32), that non-Christians will take note of their moral integrity.

Besides urging congregations to display an integrity that commends Jesus to unbelievers, Paul in 1 Cor 14 tells Corinth's congregation to rethink its worship, since worship is not just a gathering of believers but an entry point for "outsiders" or "unbelievers" to hear the gospel. For Paul, congregations are not private clubs. Had first-century congregations been so, they would have been left undisturbed; that is not what happened. To the contrary, congregations for Paul are to be local, public, corporate agents of God's mission, leading him to write in 2 Cor 3:2–3: "You yourselves are our letter, written on our hearts, to be known and read by all; and you show that you are a letter of Christ, prepared by us, written not with ink but with the Spirit of the living God, not on tablets of stone but on tablets of human hearts."

In all cultures, a letter is a means of communication. So is a congregation, says Paul, though not written in ink. "You are a letter of Christ," he told Corinth's congregation—your corporate life is meant to communicate Christ. Paul inferred this missional purpose in his opening salutation to Corinth's *ekklesia*: "To the church of God that is in Corinth, to those who are sanctified in Christ Jesus, called to be saints" (1 Cor 1:2). Naming Corinth's congregation as "sanctified" and "saints," Jewish words for those set apart for God's service, Paul links his call to Corinth's congregation to that of Israel to be a holy people and a light to the nations. Quoting Lev 19:2 ("You shall be holy [*hagioi*], for I the Lord your God am holy [*hagios*]"), Richard Hays adds that in applying this language to the Corinthians, Paul echoes "God's call to Israel [and] implicitly addresses and describes the Corinthian Christians . . . as members of the covenant people of God . . . . Whatever their background, they have now been caught up into the story of God's gracious elective purpose . . . representing God's kingdom within a world that does not know God."[21]

Hays's comments return us to the "in Christ" identity of congregations, which I will briefly summarize by looking at some of the prepositions the New Testament uses to link congregations to Jesus. I begin with a text where Paul tells Colossae's congregation,

> [Christ] is the image of the invisible God, the firstborn of all creation; for in him all things in heaven and on earth were created, things visible and invisible, whether thrones or dominions or rulers or powers—all things have been created through him and for

---

21. Hays, *First Corinthians*, 16.

him. He himself is before all things, and in him all things hold together. He is the head of the body, the church; he is the beginning, the firstborn from the dead, so that he might come to have first place in everything. For in him all the fullness of God was pleased to dwell, and through him God was pleased to reconcile to himself all things . . . by making peace through the blood of his cross. (Col 1:15–20)

This text links Colossae's congregation to Jesus and highlights its dependence on him. After all, says Paul, "all things have been created through him and for him . . . in him all things hold together . . . in him all the fullness of God was pleased to dwell . . . through him God was pleased to reconcile to himself all things" (Col 1:15–20). According to N. T. Wright, here Paul helps a congregation to grow in confidence by clarifying that Jesus is supreme: "The more they get to know, and know about, Jesus Christ, the more they will understand who the true God is and what he's done; who they are as a result; and what it means to live in and for him."[22]

In the Col 1 text just quoted, Paul uses various prepositions to stress the dependency of believers and congregations on Jesus. One of them is *for*, frequently used in Paul's letters. He told Corinth's congregation, for example, that "Christ died *for* our sins" (1 Cor 15:3; emphasis mine) and at 2 Cor 5:21 wrote, "*for* our sake [God] made Christ to be sin, so that in him we might become the righteousness of God" (emphasis mine). He told Rome's congregation, "If God is *for* us, who is against us? He who did not withhold his own Son, but gave him up *for* all of us, will he not with him also give us everything else?" (Rom 8:31; emphasis mine). The preposition *for* conveys Paul's conviction that before all else, congregations of believers are debtors to God's grace. As debtors to the God who is for us and who sent his Son to die for us, no one, Paul tells Corinth's conflicted congregation, has the right to "boast in the presence of God" (1 Cor 1:29). Paul rebukes the inflated claims to social status, wisdom, and spiritual superiority made by Corinth's factions by placing Jesus, who "died for all, so that those who live might live no longer for themselves but for him who died and was raised for them" (2 Cor 5:15) at the core of congregational identity.

Another key Pauline preposition is *through*. If Heb 1:1–2 presents Jesus as the one *through* whom God came to us—"in these last days he has spoken to us by a Son"—Paul presents Jesus as the one *through* whom we come to God; as he wrote at Col 1:20, just quoted, "through [Christ] God

---

22. Wright, *Paul for Everyone*, 150.

was pleased to reconcile to himself all things ... by making peace through the blood of the cross." Similarly, Paul told Corinth's congregation, "All this is from God, who reconciled us to himself through Christ" (2 Cor 5:18). Believers, congregations, and indeed the world depend on God's grace mediated through Christ if they are to be reconciled to God. Paul states this in Rom 3:22–25: "There is no distinction, since all have sinned and fall short of the glory of God; they are now justified by his grace as a gift, through the redemption that is in Christ Jesus, whom God put forward as a sacrifice of atonement by his blood, effective through faith."

Because God is our gracious redeemer, none can justify themselves before God by their work or wisdom, a truth with which Paul confronted Corinth's congregational factions: "Since, in the wisdom of God, the world did not know God through wisdom, God decided through our proclamation of" "Jesus Christ and him crucified" (1 Cor 2:2) "to save those who believe" (1 Cor 1:21). Paul's consistent response to congregational problems was to focus on Jesus.

Though only alluded to in 1 Cor 3, Paul also uses the preposition *on*, which shows up in a story about Paul found in Acts 16, a text about the conversion of Paul's jailer in Philippi. The jailer, asking Paul and Silas what he must do to be saved, received this reply: "Believe on the Lord Jesus Christ" (Acts 16:30). If individual believers are to believe in Christ, congregations must build on Christ, a point that Paul makes in 1 Cor 3 when he refers to the foundation on which Corinth's congregation was built. The congregation was fighting over various church leaders, with some congregants claiming, "I belong to Paul," "I belong to Apollos," "I belong to Cephas," or "I belong to Christ" (1 Cor 1:11–12). It may be that each Corinthian faction championed a different leader, but whatever the case, Paul was scandalized. "Was Paul crucified for you? Or were you baptized in the name of Paul?" (1 Cor 1:13). Paul's response acknowledges that human leaders can help congregations but insists that "no one can lay any foundation other than the one that has been laid; that foundation is Jesus Christ" (1 Cor 3:11).

In his Corinthian letters, Paul consistently draws Corinth's congregation away from its own drama to its "in Christ" identity. In dealing with that congregation's pressures and personalities, Paul insists that a congregation stands in need of Christ's grace. In their book *When Church Stops Working*, Andrew Root and Blair Bertrand say something similar. Written for North America's now deflated congregations rather than Corinth's long-ago inflated congregation, Root and Bertrand claim that "the church is essential, but only as it realizes and confesses that it is not the star of its own story. The church can be faithful only when its focus is not on its own actions but on the acts of God . . . Jesus who lives, bringing life out of death."[23]

Now to the preposition *in*, one that Paul frequently uses in his phrase "in Christ," which John Mackay suggests is "the central category of Paul's thinking."[24] Believers (2 Cor 12:2) and congregations in Christ, even Corinth's (1 Cor 1:2), partake of a new reality, says Paul. Having participated in Adam's disobedience, which brought death into the world, believers now participate in Christ's sin-defeating death that brings life—"in Christ there is a new creation" (2 Cor 5:17). Accordingly, Christians not only have "a new status and . . . a new source of strength," writes Mackay, but they are those "in whom a new principle of life has been implanted," such that Christ is "the soil in which they grow, the atmosphere which they breathe, the source and goal of their entire existence."[25]

Paul further defines the "in Christ" identity of congregations in Rom 6:5–11: "If we have been united with him in a death like his, we will certainly be united with him in a resurrection like his. We know that our old self was crucified with him so that the body of sin might be destroyed, and we might no longer be enslaved to sin . . . you also must consider yourselves dead to sin and alive to God in Christ Jesus." Charles Cranfield comments that Rome's believers were "in Christ" because of "God's decision as our gracious Judge to see us, not as we are in ourselves, but 'in Him.' Our being in Christ is a matter . . . of a divine decision . . . God accepts Christ's death as having been for us and His risen life as being lived for us."[26] Yet it ought to be added that alongside God's objective decision for us, believers must subjectively die to sin and be spiritually renewed, a process that Paul expected even in Corinth's flawed congregation.

One more comment on the "in Christ" identity of congregations: Richard Hays writes that "for Jews like Paul, the Jerusalem temple had been understood as the central focus of the divine presence in the world. Thus, when Paul transfers this claim to the community of predominantly gentile Christians in Corinth, he is making a world-shattering hermeneutical move . . . . The Spirit of God no longer can be localized in a sacred building: it is to be

---

23. Root and Bertrand, *When Church Stops Working*, 77.
24. Mackay, *God's Order*, 97.
25. Mackay, *God's Order*, 99.
26. Cranfield, *Critical and Exegetical Commentary*, 316.

found in the gathered community of God's elect people in Christ."[27] Few North American congregations call themselves a "gathered community of God's elect people in Christ," yet that is how the New Testament thinks of congregations. It respects congregations by taking seriously that an *ekklesia* is a community of God's people that is joined to and living in Christ, an identity that Paul assumes in the following text: "Blessed be the God and Father of our Lord Jesus Christ, who has blessed us in Christ . . . [and] chose us in Christ . . . . In him we have redemption through his blood, the forgiveness of our trespasses . . . . In Christ we have also obtained an inheritance" (Eph 1:3, 4, 7, 11). Alive in Christ, a congregation can never be what I once heard someone call it—a Sweet Jesus Memorial Society!

Corinth's believers, however, failed to recognize that their congregation participated in the cosmic new life drama begun by Christ (2 Cor 5:17) who, for Paul, is the power and wisdom of God (1 Cor 1:24) and the mystery and glory of God (1 Cor 2:1, 8) who will one day hand over "the kingdom to God the Father, after he has destroyed every ruler and every authority and power. For he must reign until he has put all his enemies under his feet" (1 Cor 15:24). But does not Paul's awareness of Corinth's troubled congregation contradict the grand theological and missional identity he gives it? Aware that the congregation didn't fully respect what it was in Christ, Paul addressed 1 Corinthians to "infants in Christ" not "spiritual people" (1 Cor 3:1), yet he did not do what some congregational leaders do—ease the contradiction between a congregation's identity and practice by diluting the former to suit the latter. Paul told Corinth's *ekklesia*, built on Christ and indwelt by the Spirit, that though a work in progress, it lacked no "spiritual gift as you wait for the revealing of our Lord Jesus Christ" (1 Cor 1:7). To respect a congregation is to affirm such an identity and anticipate such an outcome.

If, as the apostle Paul insists, congregations are caught up into the risen life of Jesus, I suspect that many current North American congregations are so taken up with their "in Corinth" issues that they cannot fully grasp their "in Christ" identity. But this was also true of New Testament congregations; indeed, it was the difficulty that congregations had in living out both their "in Corinth" and "in Christ" identities that prompted New Testament authors to write what they did, says Darrell Guder: "The apostolic strategy of continuing formation of missional communities became the motivation of their writings . . . these Scriptures . . . deal with the

---

27. Hays, *First Corinthians*, 57.

problems and the conflicts, the challenges and the doubts as they emerged in particular contexts, so that these communities could be faithful."[28]

Accordingly, Paul wrote 1 Corinthians to help a congregation to navigate life in a multi-religious city, confronting some congregational members who took other members to court over trivial matters, and calling other congregational members to resist indulging in the city's sexual deviancy and to live as people "washed, sanctified and justified in the name of the Lord Jesus" (1 Cor 6:11). Paul refused to dilute the "in Christ" identity of Corinth's congregation to make its life easier "in Corinth."

Life is far from easy for current North American congregations, which is why some are tempted to dilute their "in Christ" identity to make their lives in a secular culture easier, and others are tempted to retreat from a secular culture in an effort to preserve their "in Christ" identity. In either case, such congregations betray what lies at the heart of God's mission— that "the Word became flesh and blood, and moved into the neighborhood" (John 1:14 MSG). John's point is that in Jesus, glory met grit, and eternity intersected a local time and place. That incarnational principle, denoted by my highlighting of the "in Corinth" and "in Christ" identities of a congregation, is what current congregations are called to respect, no matter how challenging that may be.

First Corinthians proceeds to address how the failure of Corinth's congregation to respect its "in Christ" identity impacted its life and especially its worship. Anthony Thiselton titles the section of his commentary devoted to chapters 11–14 of 1 Corinthians as "Mutual Respect in Matters of Public Worship." Paul opens chapter 11 by discussing head covering in worship since, it seems, some female leaders refused to cover their heads during worship in a bid for gender equality with men. Though he professed gender equality in Gal 3:28—"there is no longer Jew or Greek, there is no longer slave or free, there is no longer male or female; for all of you are one in Christ Jesus"—and promoted the equality of men and women as worship leaders in Corinth, Paul worried that attempts to abolish gender distinction in the church might compromise the congregation's witness. While approving the freedom of women to publicly pray and preach, Paul was unhappy, says Thiselton, "about any assumption that gender equality means gender sameness or gender interchangeability, and even more unhappy about their indifference to the principle of respect and respectability."[29]

28. Guder, *Called to Witness*, 91–92.
29. Thiselton, *First Corinthians*, 173.

Respecting Congregations

What women wear on their head during worship isn't a current issue, but congregational respect is, leading Thiselton to say that respect for "the other" is the keynote of 1 Cor 11:1–16, whether "for God, for fellow Christians at worship, for the Roman world as it perceives Christians."[30] First Corinthians 11 illustrates that disrespect in congregations often arises not from heresy but from what is inappropriate. That is still true within contemporary congregations. Consider a church organist whose eccentric playing disables the congregation's ability to praise God; consider a choir so intent on singing its anthems in nonvernacular languages that it is difficult for a congregation to receive a message from or respond to God through those anthems; consider a praise band whose rock style drowns out congregational singing. None of these examples is heretical, yet they all disrespect congregational participation in worship. Or consider a pastor who ignores emails and phone messages left by congregants, and who thinks of congregational home visits as wasting time having tea with old ladies. Though not heretical, this behavior disrespects a congregation hoping to know and be known by its pastor.

Disappointed by dissension in Corinth's congregation over headdress, Paul was even more distressed by how the congregation celebrated the Lord's Supper. He wrote, "I hear that there are divisions among you . . . For when the time comes to eat, each of you goes ahead with your own supper, and one goes hungry, and another becomes drunk" (1 Cor 11:18, 21). It seems that at the Supper, then celebrated as part of a larger meal in the homes of well-off members, high-status believers ate in a dining room while lower status believers stood beyond it. Such social differentiation meant that some got drunk while others remained hungry. Angry that Corinth's contest for status was affecting congregational life, Paul accused the congregation's elitist faction of showing "contempt for the church of God" by using pagan definitions to evaluate who was to be honored and who was not (1 Cor 11:22). Paul expected the congregation, understood as God's temple and indwelt by God's Spirit, to resist such elitism; after all, every congregant had been "baptized into one body—Jews and Greeks, slaves or free" and had been "made to drink of one Spirit" (1 Cor 12:13).

Responding to the failure of Corinth's congregation to respect its identity in Christ, Paul enlarged that identity by calling the congregation "the body of Christ." After telling his Corinthian converts to flee the worship of idols, Paul used the phrase as he wrote of the Lord's Supper: "The cup of

---

30. Thiselton, *First Corinthians*, 179.

blessing that we bless, is it not a sharing in the blood of Christ? The bread that we break, is it not a sharing in the body of Christ? Because there is one bread, we who are many are one body" (1 Cor 10:16). Richard Hays suggests that here Paul has in mind the widely held view that sacred meals had power to create "a relation of *koinonia* ["fellowship"] among participants and between participants and the deity honored in the meal."[31] If so, participants at the Lord's Supper not only express allegiance to Jesus by partaking of one bread (1 Cor 10:17), but each believer, joined to Christ by faith and by sacrament, joins other believers to form one body. Addressed to congregational factions claiming to belong to Paul, Apollos, Cephas, and Christ, Paul's "one body" phrase stressed the congregation's corporate identity in Christ and its common commitment to Christ, whom Paul in Eph 1:22 names as "the head over all things for the church, which is his body."

Having called the congregation "the body of Christ," Paul goes on to warn the congregation that "all who eat and drink without discerning the body, eat and drink judgment against themselves" (1 Cor 11:29). That text, traditionally read as referring to Christ's crucified body, is read by recent interpreters who take "the body" as a reference to the congregation, and as confirming, writes Robert Banks, "the high estimate Paul had of the local Christian community."[32] If so, Paul tells Corinth's congregants that to eat the bread and drink the cup together was to realize their corporate union in Christ, whose body and blood the bread and cup signified. United as the body of Christ, factions thus had no place in the congregation, and no member must shame another, for such contempt disrespects the congregation as the body of Christ, profanes the Supper, and is liable to incur judgment.

In 1 Cor 11 and 12, Paul draws Corinth's congregation away from its internal squabbling by emphasizing its identity as "the body of Christ," a phrase that promotes both congregational unity and diversity. Like a human body, a congregation is one, yet it has many parts and many spiritual gifts. But at the same time, Paul insists that the congregation's diverse spiritual gifts are for "the common good" of the body, not to enhance personal status (1 Cor 12:7). He presses the idea of the congregation being one body while aware that Corinth's congregants had little natural affinity with each other—Greeks and Jews, slaves and free, are mentioned in 1 Cor 12:13. For Paul, far from being a club of like-minded people, a congregation is a body that has the spiritual power to overcome divisions, which in North America would

---

31. Hays, *First Corinthians*, 167.
32. Banks, *Paul's Idea of Community*, 63.

include divisions rooted in race, linguistics, economic status, and gender. For this to be so, congregational respect is required!

Paul enlarges his "body of Christ" metaphor as 1 Cor 12 proceeds, urging that as one body, the congregation has no unneeded extra body part. Yet some congregational members in Corinth felt that they were unneeded extras. At 12:15–16, Paul imagines their thinking: "If the foot would say, 'Because I am not a hand, I do not belong to the body,' that would not make it any less a part of the body. And if the ear would say, 'Because I am not an eye, I do belong to the body,' that would not make it any less a part of the body." To reassure disrespected members, Paul corrects the disrespect of elitist members in 12:21–23: "The eye cannot say to the hand, 'I have no need of you,' nor again the head to the feet, 'I have no need of you.' On the contrary, the members of the body that seem to be weaker are indispensable, and those members of the body that we think less honorable we clothe with greater honor and our less respectable members . . . with greater respect." Confronting the contempt of some congregants for others, Paul pleads with Corinth's congregation to respect its diversity but also its unique "one body in Christ" identity.

Paul's teaching on congregational identity was revolutionary. In a slave-owning society, the idea of removing barriers between slave and free was unthinkable, yet Paul expects that to happen in congregations as slaves and slaveowners share the Lord's Supper. He told Corinth's congregation, "In the one Spirit we were all baptized into one body—Jews and Greeks, slaves and free" (1 Cor 12:13) and told the Galatians, "There is no longer Jew or Greek . . . slave or free . . . male and female; for all of you are one in Christ Jesus" (Gal 3:28). Even the apostle Peter, as Paul himself knew, stumbled over the revolutionary implications of Jew and gentile being one in Christ (see Gal 2:11–12) within one body, whose diverse members had been baptized by one Spirit and had confessed one Lord.

Scholars say that Paul borrowed his "body of Christ" phrase from Greek political rhetoric, where it was used to protect the unity of a patrician-ruled society from plebeian protests seeking to upset the status quo. However, writes Margaret Mitchell, Paul uses body language "not to keep subordinates in their place but to urge the members of the community to respect and value . . . those who appeared to be their inferiors."[33] The diversity and unity of a congregation is enhanced when the "respectable" parts

---

33. Mitchell, *Rhetoric of Reconciliation*, 183.

of the body respect its "less respectable parts," says 1 Cor 12:23–24, which allows a congregation to respect those whom the world despises.[34]

CONCLUSION

Most of what I have written about congregational identity has been drawn from 1 Corinthians, but I will take note of one more text, Acts 2:37–47, which describes the congregation that formed after the Pentecost Day preaching of the apostle Peter. This new congregation's life was marked by worship, named in the breaking of bread, in prayer, and in awe among believers in the temple and their homes (Acts 2:42, 46); its life was marked by fellowship as believers sold and shared possessions and distributed "the proceeds to all, as any had need" (Acts 2:45); its life was marked by discipleship as new believers devoted themselves to "the apostles' teaching" (Acts 2:42); and its life was marked by scattered outreach, which led to the congregation enjoying "the good will of all the people" and the Lord adding daily "to their number those who were being saved" (Acts 2:47). Though descriptive rather than prescriptive, this text strongly suggests the identity, purpose, and priorities of New Testament congregations, to which I will return in chapters 4 and 5.

Now, three last thoughts. First, it is fair to say that a congregation forms and grows when believers choose to join forces or when new believers join an already existing congregation, but it is also true that a text like Acts 2:47 attributes congregational formation to God—"day by day the Lord added to their number." As Paul told Corinth's congregation, "God decided through the foolishness of our proclamation to save those who believe . . . He is the source of your life in Christ" (1 Cor 1:21–22). The idea of God as the source of congregations is also reflected in Jesus telling his disciples, "You did not choose me; I chose you" (John 15:16). But do North American congregations believe that it is God who builds congregations? Or is a congregation thought of as a project undertaken by clergy with the energy and charisma to grow it? I will return to this issue.

Second, while New Testament congregations were expected to be socially inclusive, they at the same time made exclusive claims about Jesus. This inclusive-exclusive congregational identity, even if imperfectly fulfilled, challenged the socially divided, religiously pluralist world of Paul's day. Today, however, the combined inclusive-exclusive identity of New

---

34. Thiselton, *First Corinthians*, 992.

Testament congregations is not often apparent in North America, where congregations that aspire to social inclusivity are tempted to avoid the exclusivity of the New Testament's claims about Jesus, and where congregations that defend the exclusivity of the New Testament's claims about Jesus are tempted to avoid rather than advance any social inclusivity. This leads to a question: To what extent do current congregations respect the identity that the New Testament offers them? This is a question that the next chapter will address.

Third, my call for congregations to respect the identity that the New Testament gives to them is likely to raise this question: Is what the New Testament said about congregations two millennia ago relevant to North America's twenty-first-century congregations? Some of what the New Testament says about congregations relates to their cultural conditions then and cannot be simply transferred to the cultural conditions of current congregations: Paul's discussion in 1 Cor 11 of what women wear on their heads during worship is one example; another is the advice Paul gives in Eph 6 to slaves and masters who belonged to the same congregation. Let's just say that interpreting the Bible requires careful discernment, yet in almost every time and place, the church has read the Bible as normative for its life. Thinking of the Bible as the story of Israel and then Jesus Christ, Stephen Farris writes, "for us Christians this story is uniquely privileged in that by it we measure all other words and indeed actions to ascertain whether they might indeed come from God.... The Bible, then, is the 'identity story' of the church.... It is not our own; it comes to us as a voice from beyond."[35] I agree with that statement and thus take with the utmost seriousness what the New Testament says about congregations.

---

35. Farris, *Preaching that Matters*, 3–5.

3

The Challenge Involved in Respecting Congregations

RESPECTING THE IDENTITY THAT the New Testament articulates for congregations has long been and remains a challenge for North American congregations. To understand why, I go back to the 1950s, when leading a congregation was quite different from now. In the 1950s, clergy preached twice on Sunday, ensured that a Sunday school was staffed, visited church families, invited new folk in town to attend church, and maybe taught a religion class in a local school. Protestant clergy often took their pastoral cues from Andrew Blackwood, a professor at Princeton Seminary from 1930 to 1950. His books reflect an era when churches were well attended, clergy were respected, and cultural norms were largely uncontested. Blackwood's 1949 book, *Pastoral Leadership*, genially urged clergy to promote household religion, Christian nurture, evangelism, community betterment, and world missions, while exalting the church, leading worship, preaching the gospel, teaching the people, giving private counsel, and planning and praying for all of that in their study.[1] Far from reflecting the threat of the Second World War or Cold War, Blackwood's books assume stable congregations within a stable Christendom.

---

1. Blackwood, *Pastoral Leadership*, 19–20.

THE IMPACT OF THE 1960S ON CONGREGATIONS

During the 1960s cultural revolution in North America, Blackwood's world evaporated; as the authority of mainline Protestant clergy ebbed away, so did the privileges of the congregations they served. In 2012, Matthew Engel described the impact of the 1960s revolution in one witty sentence: "Everything was about to happen. Yeah, yeah, yeah, but no one saw it coming . . . Sexual intercourse would not just be invented but would catch on big time."[2] The 1960s youth-led revolution rejected 1950s-style social conformity and resisted the long-established authority of parents, government, military, and church. Among the cultural forces at work were demands for racial justice, reflected in America's civil rights marches, and echoed in the civil unrest in Northern Ireland, my province of birth. Led by educated Catholics tired of being dismissed by a Protestant majority, Irish students joined students around the globe to protest injustice and war. As they did so, students left conventional congregational respectability far behind. Though few 1960s congregations became hotbeds of radicalism, an authority-questioning mood took hold of that decade's youth; changed their hairstyles, hemlines, and habits; and left them caught between churchgoing parents and church-dismissive peers.

By the end of the 1960s, many of those baptized in the 1950s had dropped out of church. During the 1950s, membership in Canada's mainline denominations kept growing before peaking in 1964, and American church statistics show a similar pattern. But there were already signs of unease. In 1953, John Mackay, then-president of Princeton Seminary, wrote that "we live in the Post-Constantine age, a time in which the imposing unity of Church and State has been shattered."[3] Another symptom of pre-1960s unease was the attempt to turn Protestant clergy into counsellors who were to use insights from psychology and psychotherapy,[4] attempts never contemplated by Andrew Blackwood. Overnight, it seemed, avant-garde case-study methods were promoted in clinical pastoral education courses, and they became the new source of pastoral insight, leading some to wonder if the sermons, songs, and sacraments of local congregations were still effective.

---

2. Engel, "1962."
3. Mackay, *God's Order*, 19.
4. Michaelsen, "Protestant Ministry in America," 289.

The Challenge Involved in Respecting Congregations

Not everyone welcomed such ministry experimentation. James Smart, a professor at Union Seminary, New York, complained in 1960 that American individualism was encouraging clergy to feel "free as Christian ministers to make of the ministry whatever" they wished. We're not free to reinvent ministry, said Smart; rather, we must "grasp with the utmost clarity the character of Jesus's ministry [and] submit our ministries to his that he may fulfil his ministry in us."[5] Though Smart didn't deny that psychotherapy and psychology might help clergy, he told them not to drop preaching, teaching, and pastoral care priorities to become "a species of amateur psychiatrist."[6]

That said, most Protestant clergy in the 1960s, despite the era's cultural changes, continued to serve conventional congregations. I recall my Irish Presbyterian minister railing against rock groups calling themselves the Animals, the Monkees, or the Beatles. Meanwhile, some of America's progressive clergy did experiment with new therapeutic skills within their congregations; some radical clergy became antiracist and antiwar activists beyond their congregations; and some others, fascinated by the avant-garde theologians who said that God was dead, or if alive was to be found in the tumult of the city rather than in tedious congregations, left their congregations.[7]

My sense is that North American congregations have, since the 1960s, struggled to come to terms with the loss of prestige and power they enjoyed during the era we call Christendom, an era in which Western society gave social and legal support not only to Europe's state churches but to North America's voluntary churches. Some clergy, sensing their loss of privilege, clung to the past; others cast tradition aside in search of an exciting new church future. Protectors and protestors of the status quo found little to approve in each other.

That same dynamic, of course, impacted other areas of cultural life beyond the church, one being a field I once considered as a career—urban planning. In the 1960s, urban planning changed radically, as huge highways and high-rise housing schemes replaced old neighborhoods, some of them slums. However, in 1971, a highway being built to connect Toronto's expanding suburbs to its downtown was stopped in its tracks by wealthy citizens trying to protect their leafy enclaves. They were joined by Jane Jacobs, who had protested massive urban renewal in New York City

---

5. Smart, *Rebirth of Ministry*, 19 and 37.
6. Smart, *Rebirth of Ministry*, 120.
7. Quinley, *Prophetic Clergy*, 17.

led by Robert Moses, the city's Commissioner of Parks. Neither a protector of privilege nor opposed in principle to urban renewal, Jacobs argued nevertheless that modernist, rationalist urban planning, eager to demolish slums and "start over," disrespected older communities and older people. In her classic book, *The Death and Life of Great American Cities*, she wrote scathingly that "planners frequently seem to be less well equipped intellectually for respecting and understanding particulars than ordinary people, untrained in expertise."[8] In times of radical change, and the 1960s was such a time, disrespect for what is old often prevails. This zeitgeist hugely impacted congregational life.

Despite the cultural changes, student protests, and race riots of the 1960s, seen on television by millions, most congregations—ethnic, Catholic, evangelical, charismatic, and mainline—survived. And yet Anthony Robinson's book *Transforming Congregational Culture* claims that congregations lost their traditional purpose and were ill-prepared to address that era's political scandals, new immigration patterns, rising divorce rates, drugs, and war. He summarizes the traditional purpose of congregations as being the conscience of the community, local instruments of aid, and centers for family and community life. Those roles were valuable, but mainline congregations, says Robinson, were so attuned to North American culture "that any tension between gospel and culture was diminished or lost."[9] Besides, the church as conscience of the community tended toward moralism; the church as instrument of aid masked the fact that aid-giving Christians also needed God's mercy, and by the 1960s, the role of the church as center for community and family life was being diluted by divorce and the diverse living patterns of urban America. More concerning, adds Robinson, the civic faith of mainline congregations was not distinctively Christian: "It was difficult to tell the difference between a Christian way of life and the American and middle-class way of life . . . . That worked pretty well until people began to say . . . 'If that's all it means, why do I need the church?'"[10]

Robinson's summary of civic faith may have held sway in the 1960s in his denomination, the United Church of Christ, but it is too "civic" for the Presbyterian Church in Canada, where gospel preaching; the centrality of Jesus Christ; and the raising of children in the nurture and admonition of the Lord through Sunday schools, vacation Bible schools, youth ministry,

---

8. Jacobs, *Death and Life*, 441.
9. Robinson, *Transforming Congregational Culture*, 30.
10. Robinson, *Transforming Congregational Culture*, 31.

The Challenge Involved in Respecting Congregations

and summer camps remained key features of the denomination throughout the twentieth century. As for big-E Evangelical congregations, their evangelistic commitment to the saving of souls has long been and still remains a key purpose. Yet Robinson has a point: in the second half of the twentieth century, North America's mainline denominations prioritized cultural relevance over confessional precision, and social tolerance over evangelism, and were unprepared, he says, "to give an account of their faith to their new neighbors or even . . . to their children."[11]

Dean Kelley's 1972 book, *Why Conservative Churches Are Growing*, offered a similar assessment. Noting the numerical growth within America's evangelical congregations in contrast to numerical decline within its mainline congregations, he concluded that the latter, unable to give compelling Christian answers to life's big questions and unwilling to demand a distinctive, Christian discipleship, suffered from a "lack of seriousness."[12] At any rate, congregations with a civic faith identity and purpose declined in the latter decades of the twentieth century, leaving half-empty congregations to circle the wagons and focus on keeping their aging supporters. My hunch is that church dropouts in the 1960s and 1970s felt no need to gain respectability by attending church and despised congregations that seemed to have no greater purpose.

LATE TWENTIETH-CENTURY CALLS FOR CONGREGATIONAL CHANGE

Just when North American congregations seemed headed for the wall, a new voice heralded a new future. Lyle Schaller, an American Methodist who had been an urban planner in the 1950s, transferred his social analysis skills in the 1960s to church planning. His 1972 book, *The Change Agent*, caught the attention of clergy tired of conventional church life but suspicious of radical alternatives. Alert to congregational decline, Schaller urged church leaders to use what he called "organization development theory" to analyze and retool their congregations.[13] Genuinely concerned for the church and careful to avoid doctrinal issues, Schaller was widely welcomed, though what he offered were social rather than spiritual renewal strategies. His 1988 book, *44 Ways to Increase Church Attendance*, was typical:

11. Robinson, *Transforming Congregational Culture*, 8.
12. Kelley, *Why Conservative Churches Are Growing*, 120.
13. Schaller, *Change Agent*, 188.

It suggested involving more people, scheduling more special Sundays, and making a special summer effort since "two-thirds of all families who change their place of residence do so" during summer months.[14]

Schaller's proposals were based on well-known human behavior patterns and preferences; hence, his call that church buildings be "clean, neat, and attractive" or that sanctuary acoustics be good, since "the proportion of churchgoers who have passed their sixtieth birthday continues to climb."[15] Schaller helped congregational leaders, me included, to rethink congregational leadership; nevertheless, his untheological approach to congregations later caused me to ask what happens in the long-term to congregations that ignore their theological identity.

Schaller's books initiated a flood of resources for congregations, not least those produced by the Alban Institute. Established in 1974, Alban encouraged church leaders to use behavioral and organizational theory to rethink how congregations work. Meanwhile, a confident burgeoning evangelical movement organized church growth conferences and produced material that gave congregational leaders an array of methodologies to intensify outreach to un-churched and de-churched seekers. As the 1980s opened, new theories, new evangelistic techniques, and a new emphasis on market-driven programs were redefining what congregational life might look like.

Recipes for congregational effectiveness that treated congregations as places for significant ministry created more confident congregations. Yet evangelical approaches to evangelism and church growth, though based on the Great Commission of Matt 28 and clothed in biblical piety, were often as untheological as mainline Schaller. Consider the popular 1977 book, *Ten Steps for Church Growth*, by Donald McGavran and Win Arn, or McGavran's *Understanding Church Growth* book. Both propose an evangelistic methodology based on a sociological insight that McGavran called the "homogeneity principle," which is that it is easier to become a Christian when the challenge of changing race, class, or clan is diminished: "It takes no great acumen to see that when marked differences of color, stature, income, cleanliness, and education are present, men understand the Gospel better when expounded by their own kind of people. They prefer to join churches whose members look, talk, and act like themselves."[16]

---

14. Schaller, *44 Ways to Increase*, 73.
15. Schaller, *44 Ways to Increase*, 92 and 95.
16. McGavran, *Understanding Church Growth*, 227.

The Challenge Involved in Respecting Congregations

McGavran's strategy contradicts the "one body" yet culturally diverse congregation that the apostle Paul called for in 1 Corinthians. Be that as it may, committed to what works rather than the finer points of New Testament theology, the Church Growth Movement led by McGavran raised clergy confidence; even Canada's sober Presbyterians set a goal to double their denomination's membership in the 1980s. Also influential during the 1980s was the emergence of a cadre of entrepreneurial pastors eager to revive old congregations or start new ones, a few of which became megachurches. Canadian missiologist Alan Roxburgh captures the hope and the naivete of the time like this:

> Denominations, schools, and parachurch organizations created bands of church growth consultants who fanned out across the continent with binder-driven workshops, training events, and assessment tools to diagnose how a church could move off its plateau to the next numerical level.... Just master the binder, ignite members' spirituality, enlarge the sanctuary, fix the parking lot, or completely relocate to the crossroads where malls and housing developments were about to break ground.[17]

But as the 1980s ended, the question was asked, Were all the new evangelical and mainline strategies really fixing the late twentieth-century church? Loren Mead, founder of the Alban Institute, voiced doubt in his 1991 book, *The Once and Future Church*. Describing the death of Andrew Blackwood's Christendom world, which had privileged and protected the church, Mead stated that the church was now in a much less friendly post-Christian era, a conclusion that rang true for mainline clergy. But sobering though Mead's analysis was, his hope for congregations and their future remained: "The congregation is where people touch the church and are touched by it. It is there that ... millions of people are struggling to understand their own personal sense of mission and to get strength to pursue it. The congregation is where new people are brought into a faith-heritage that connects them to the biblical story and to the life of the people of God."[18]

In alerting congregations to their changed cultural context, Mead wrote with a respect that did not dismiss their past; other church consultants, showing less respect, urged congregations to pursue radical change rather than remain tied to two thousand years of Christian tradition. Since then, respect and change have been in conflict in church circles; while

17. Roxburgh, *Joining God, Remaking Church*, 17.
18. Mead, *Once and Future Church*, 7.

respect implies the need to slow things down, change implies the need to speed things up. In this contest, change has dominated. Among those who stridently call for change is church consultant Bill Easum:

> The challenge for leadership is to change the way we feel and think about all the stimuli that bombard us every day, not to try harder or to spend more money on things that no longer work.... We don't need a better structure; we need to change the architecture of our brain.... Before we can change the way we act, we have to change the way we feel and think. We have to change our image of reality. I want to mess with your mind! I want to help you change the way you feel and think about the word "church."[19]

Change is indeed required of Christians. As a boy I memorized the *Westminster Shorter Catechism,* whose seventeenth-century word for change was sanctification: "Whereby we are renewed in the whole man after the image of God, and are enabled more and more to die unto sin, and live unto righteousness."[20] Easum is right; it costs to let something die so that something new can be born. But if congregations are to navigate a post-Christian world, some things need to remain—worship that connects us to the church of all times and places and to a God who does not change; gospel preaching rooted in the givenness of scripture and the story of Jesus; pastoral care that responds to the yearning for meaning, belonging, and hope for which all generations have longed; and enough institutional stability to avoid chaos. I note here Jeremiah's call to keep to "the ancient paths where the good way lies" (Jer 6:16), Jesus's call to keep the Commandments (Mark 10:17), and Paul's call to "hold fast to the word of life" (Phil 2:16).

Eager for change, however, some congregations too quickly dismiss the ancient paths and set aside inherited moral and theological wisdom. Now I do not think of myself as a liturgical purist, but I do think that congregations that ignore the church's liturgical resources from the past and use only contemporary worship resources are disrespectful.

As to Easum, to his credit, both his call for change and his critique of congregations that accept their decline as inevitable while ignoring Jesus's call to go and make disciples surely spring from a commendable desire to evangelize America's unchurched millions. I share Easum's critique of mainline complacency, but I do not share his crankiness. He opens his 1993 book, *Dancing with Dinosaurs,* by calling congregations that refuse

---

19. Easum, *Leadership on the Other Side,* 41–42.
20. Quoted from *Our Confessional Heritage,* 143.

The Challenge Involved in Respecting Congregations

to change "dinosaurs," whose "necks are too stiff or their eyes too nearsighted."[21] He adds that his book uses the word "church" not "in a flattering or positive way," but to name decaying, "out of touch" congregations.[22] His negativity toward church appears in his false alternatives—that the first Christians focused on "entrance into the kingdom of God instead of a church" and that "evangelizing an area is the goal instead of building a local church."[23] Though Easum assumes that congregations will appear, how are they to avoid becoming local churches about which he seems so ambiguous? Some of the clergy who follow Easum's lead, and I have met a few, evangelize beyond their congregations while bypassing the dinosaurs within them who pay their salary. It's disrespectful!

Easum is also impatient. Typical is his comment that congregations "with a slow pace of change are no longer adequate in a fast-changing world. Structures designed to coordinate ministry are unable to cause innovation. Ministries that worked in the industrial society no longer meet the spiritual needs of people in an information society. In an age of computers, we cannot express truth in the language of a chariot age."[24] Easum's rhetoric calls for change and dismisses tradition, another word that he says he always uses negatively. Easum is partly right—we do live in a fast-changing world, but not all that is new is good, and not all that is old is bad. How different is Stanley Hauerwas's comment: "Christian communities live by memory. Our central feast is a feast of memory.... It therefore becomes crucial for Christianity to be about the formation of communities in which memory is not only a possibility but a necessity."[25]

It is not surprising that, suspicious of the past, Easum also has grave doubts about infant baptism, a practice, he says, that makes little sense to church dropouts who as infants didn't "personally" experience their baptism.[26] Easum flippantly dismisses a practice that has divided the church for centuries and engaged the church's best theological minds. Equally flippant is his notion that lay congregational leaders should study "more sociology than theology," avoid seminary, and work instead "on the staff of a large

---

21. Easum, *Dancing with Dinosaurs*, 15.
22. Easum, *Dancing with Dinosaurs*, 21.
23. Easum, *Dancing with Dinosaurs*, 46 and 108.
24. Easum, *Dancing with Dinosaurs*, 12–13.
25. Hauerwas, *Better Hope*, 182.
26. Easum, *Dancing with Dinosaurs*, 109.

congregation where they can learn functional rather than doctrinal skills."[27] Easum's strategies are not conducive to forming respectful congregations. Nevertheless, my denomination, the Presbyterian Church in Canada, invited him to speak at a 2010 conference, maybe hoping that his stridency would push Canadian Presbyterians facing bleak numerical decline to try any strategy to avoid extinction, no matter how strident.

Tod Bolsinger's 2015 book, *Canoeing the Mountains: Christian Leadership in Uncharted Territory*, offers a more thoughtful call for change. A Fuller Seminary professor, Bolsinger notes how the society the church now faces differs from that of the Christendom era. I value how aware he is of the struggles that current congregations face, yet I think he overstates his case. Bolsinger opens his book with these words: "The world in front of you is nothing like the world behind you," and adds that "all we have assumed about leading Christian organizations, all we have been trained for, is out of date."[28] This got my attention, as no doubt was intended. But though Bolsinger will excite those who love the idea of "uncharted territory," he will depress clergy whose ministry skills are apparently now obsolete. Perhaps we ought not to be shocked by Bolsinger's report that upward of fifteen hundred American pastors leave the ministry each month.[29]

Throughout his book, Bolsinger references the Lewis and Clark Expedition that Thomas Jefferson commissioned in 1794 to cross the Appalachians, follow the Mississippi and Missouri Rivers, and find the Columbia River, which was believed to lead to the Pacific Ocean. What Lewis and Clark found, however, was that the Missouri River doesn't link to the Columbia River, and that between the Missouri River and the Pacific Ocean lie the great plains and the daunting Rocky Mountains. Bolsinger's point is that Lewis and Clark had to let go of their assumptions and "reframe their entire mission. What lay before them was nothing like what was behind them."[30] Bolsinger adroitly likens the adaptations forced on Lewis and Clark to those that congregational leaders must now make—letting go of the assumptions that drove Christendom-era ministry so as to navigate the uncharted territory facing twenty-first-century congregations.

Bolsinger calls congregational leaders not to do what they have always done, and rightly challenges them to adapt, innovate, and experiment

---

27. Easum, *Dancing with Dinosaurs*, 113–12 and 124n27.
28. Bolsinger, *Canoeing the Mountains*, 17 and 28.
29. Bolsinger, *Canoeing the Mountains*, 12.
30. Bolsinger, *Canoeing the Mountains*, 27.

The Challenge Involved in Respecting Congregations

within their congregations without getting anxious! But at the risk of being pedantic, I find his call for change too absolutist. Yes, Lewis and Clark were shocked when their expedition turned out to be much longer and more challenging than expected, but they adapted the skill sets they had developed from years of past experiences, and they made their way across ground that, though extremely tough, was not totally different from that behind them; rivers were still rivers, and mountains were still mountains, even if much higher. As to North America's congregations, Bolsinger says that they live in a different world, but it isn't totally different. Some traditional areas of congregational ministry remain: the Bible still needs to be taught with fidelity, baptismal water still seals us to Jesus, and the broken bread and poured wine of the Lord's Supper still unite us to Jesus's dying and undying love.

My point is that congregations do not and cannot just live in the present; they are part of the long story of God's world mission in which the congregation of Israel and Paul's struggling congregations once took part. The fact is that every church generation experiences continuity and discontinuity as it inherits the gospel and discovers new ways to express it. Thus, every congregation has a before as well as a present. Addressed personally to Jeremiah rather than congregations, Jer 1:5 nevertheless offers them a wise word: "Before I formed you in the womb I knew you, before you were born, I set you apart; I appointed you as a prophet." Of this verse Eugene Peterson says, "Apart from the *before*, the *now* has little meaning. . . . The *before* is the root system of the visible *now*."[31] But if clergy are told that their ministry skills from *before* are of little or no value *now*, no wonder they give up.

A more respectful approach to change will recognize that congregations need the wisdom of the past to help them adapt and innovate into the future. As it happens, while Bolsinger opens his book calling for radical change, he later admits that as congregations adapt to the world in front of them, they must protect essential "theology, traditions [and] ministry practices" from the world behind them if they are to remain Christian.[32] I heartily agree; congregations untethered from the biblical Jesus will not long remain Christian.

Calls for change from less nuanced writers than Bolsinger inspire zealous risk-takers but discombobulate traditionalists. So, what are we to do? Congregational leaders should make changes only as they figure out

---

31. Peterson, *Run with the Horses*, 36.
32. Bolsinger, *Canoeing the Mountains*, 106.

and respect what a congregation is and what it is for. At this point I quote my Irish compatriot Edmund Burke, who famously cautioned those eager to embrace the radicals who led the French Revolution: "They have no respect for the wisdom of others; but they pay it off by a very full measure of confidence in their own. With them it is a sufficient motive to destroy an old scheme of things, because it is an old one. As to the new, they are in no sort of fear with regard to the duration of a building run up in haste; because duration is no object to those who think little or nothing has been done before their time."[33]

As already suggested, not all congregational leaders value the past. What Canada's declining congregations value is success measured in numbers. This makes them envy America's large churches, even though they know that post-COVID, average Sunday attendance in American congregations is now well south of one hundred. Talking of large churches leads me to Willow Creek Community Church, begun in 1975 by Bill Hybels. By 2015, Willow Creek had twenty-five thousand people attending its Sunday services, an astounding success built on a particular strategy—to turn Sunday services, set aside for centuries for the worship of believers, into seeker services for the unchurched and de-churched. Timothy Wright sums up the seeker church model that Willow Creek made a global phenomenon in these oft-quoted words: "No spires. No crosses. No robes. No clerical collars. No hard pews. No kneelers. No biblical gobbledegook. No prayerly rote. No fire, no brimstone . . . No forced solemnity . . . Centuries of . . . habit . . . abandoned, clearing the way for new . . . forms of worship."[34]

Across North America, congregations of all sorts have adopted Willow Creek's strategy, one that bypasses much of what has long linked congregations to the rich resources of Christian history. Willow Creek did, however, strategically retain one historic tradition: the habit of people going to church on Sunday morning. That said, Willow Creek did not use traditional church time to invite believers to traditional worship—sacraments are not celebrated at Sunday services—but to invite nonbelievers and church dropouts to turn or return to God. Willow Creek's commitment to evangelism is commendable, given that such a commitment is rare in mainline circles, but this raises a big question: If Sunday services focus on evangelizing unbelievers, what happens to worship? Though evangelistic presentations can evoke worship, evangelism language talks *about* God while worship

---

33. Burke, *Reflections on the Revolution*, 57.
34. Quoted in Long, *Beyond the Worship Wars*, 27.

The Challenge Involved in Respecting Congregations

language talks *to* God. So, do seeker strategies disrespect worship? I ask, given that, as noted in the previous chapter, 1 Cor 12 and Acts 2 portray believers meeting for worship that was meant to form them to witness to unbelievers beyond worship.

It would be disrespectful not to assume that behind Willow Creek's success lies real prayer, worship, and significant spiritual passion, all of which is not always present in run-of-the-mill mainline congregations. Yet the multiple thousands who attend Willow Creek's Sunday seeker services do not participate in its mid-week opportunities for worship. Theologian Scot McKnight, a former congregant at Willow Creek, offers us insight about the congregation:

> *Relevancy* to contemporary concerns—from politics to marriage to family to finances to moral challenges—would be the door to evangelism, while it would also, ironically, turn platformed speakers into authentic humans with real struggles and pains and depressions and doubt . . . . Instead of preaching through books of the Bible, which was the custom of many evangelical churches and the heart of seminary-trained preaching classes, Hybels went after . . . *hot topics*. The audience was no longer sinners or saints but seekers, people wondering about God. So, what was attractive and inoffensive to the seeker, instead of the churchgoer, determined the content of the talks from the platform.[35]

Much that is good came to congregations that adopted a seeker church model; after hearing Easum or Hybels speak at a high-energy conference, some pastors returned to their congregations and implemented their strategies, and people came to faith in Jesus. But what sometimes followed is that the members of many small, traditional congregations—only half of whom regularly attended—resisted the pastor's radical worship changes, leading the pastor to seek a new and more appreciative congregation.

It is hard to balance respect for what is with the need to change it. Some who resist change would rather their congregation die; some who love change think their readiness to pay the price of change makes their cause godly. Unsurprisingly, change causes conflict in congregations, especially when leaders refuse to seek a respectful path between what must change and what ought not. A congregation requires routine if it is to innovate but equally requires innovation to avoid stagnation. Change can release congregational vitality, but in careless hands it can cause congregational collapse.

---

35. McKnight, "Church History and Lessons/Warnings," paras. 3–4.

Just as children, if constantly told by parents that they must change, will resent being judged as failures, so will churchgoers scolded by clergy. I have no easy answers for this conundrum, but I do think that calls for change receive a more positive response if they proceed not from slick church growth strategies, but from a respectful obedience for what God's word says about a congregation's identity, purpose, and ministry pattern.

RESPONSES TO CONGREGATIONAL FIXING STRATEGIES

Calls for change dominate the debate about the future of North America's congregations; perhaps idealist Christian leaders prefer to reimagine the future than to study the past. But as the Oxford theologian Alister McGrath says, the church, irretrievably tied to the past, is aided by tradition to remain faithful to the gospel: "Contemporary Western culture is dominated by an ideology of the ephemeral, based upon philosophies and values which are not expected to endure more than a decade or so. To take the 'great tradition' seriously is to anchor oneself to a community of reflection . . . and thus to be enriched, nourished, and above all given *stability*."[36] Respectful congregational leaders will take McGrath seriously as they allow the Spirit to lead them forward.

Respect for congregations isn't about retaining the status quo, but it does call us to appreciate the past as we live into the unknown future and calls us to see that what works in congregations aligns with biblical priorities and practices. I find this wise approach in the work of Eugene Peterson. His book *Working the Angles* critiques the program-oriented marketing approaches to congregations prevalent in the 1980s:

> American pastors are abandoning their posts, left and right, and at an alarming rate. They are not leaving their churches and getting other jobs . . . . But they are abandoning their posts, their *calling* . . . . The pastors of America have metamorphosed into a company of shopkeepers, and the shops they keep are churches. They are preoccupied with shopkeeper's concerns—how to keep the customers happy, how to lure customers away from competitors down the street, how to package the goods so that the customers will lay out more money . . . . The marketing strategies of the

---

36. McGrath, *Mere Theology*, 14.

fast-food franchise occupy the waking minds of these entrepreneurs; while asleep they dream of . . . success.[37]

For Peterson, pastors must not use consumerist definitions of success but must instead connect the "great realities of God and the great realities of salvation to the . . . parish";[38] rather than use gimmicks, they should slow down their activism and intercede between the wreckage of human lives and the reality of God's grace. Peterson's respect for God, and his respect for the tough times the church now faces, leads him to reject pastoral leadership based on pressure to fix things; instead, he says, "There is a . . . leisurely center to existence where God must be deeply pondered, lovingly believed. This demand is not for prayer-on-the-run or for prayer-on-request. It means entering realms of spirit where wonder and adoration have space to develop."[39]

Though Peterson knew that congregations must change, he resisted leadership driven by change; rather, he called leaders to listen to scripture that reorients "culture-conditioned and job-oriented assumptions and procedures . . . and calls into question the domesticated accommodations we are busily arranging for the gospel."[40] In contrast to congregational leaders who pay scant attention to how scripture portrays the identity and purposes that congregations have in God's economy, Peterson's careful respect for scripture finds within it another approach to congregational ministry. But even if his imaginative reading of scripture was well received across the church, I am not sure that Peterson's critique of consumerist church growth techniques led congregational leaders to give up the search for new strategic fixes.

Douglas Webster, offering a similar critique to Peterson's in his 1992 book, *Selling Jesus*, decries the claims of church growth gurus that marketing the church is acceptable because it seems "to be the only alternative to a church stuck in the past, resistant to change and ineffective in proclaiming and living the gospel."[41] He admits that some traditional congregations are stuck, do resist change, and have "a habit of mind that excuses mediocrity,"[42] yet Webster suggests that the urge for pastors to start congregations from

---

37. Peterson, *Working the Angles*, 1.
38. Peterson, *Working the Angles*, 11.
39. Peterson, *Working the Angles*, 45–46.
40. Peterson, *Working the Angles*, 90.
41. Webster, *Selling Jesus*, 33.
42. Webster, *Selling Jesus*, 55.

scratch rather than work with existing ones capitulates to a baby-boomer consumerist mentality. Of those who market the church, he asks provocatively "whether insight into the mind and culture of the baby-boomer generation leads to a prophetic penetration of this market niche with the gospel or promotes a culturally compatible affirmation of the culture. Does the gospel of the market-driven church redeem the lost or reinforce trends, deliver from sin or affirm the self, reconcile people to God or appeal to religious consumers?"[43]

In the decades prior to the end of the twentieth century, the marketing of congregations seemed to be working. While mainline congregations continued to decline, evangelical congregations did not. Dean Kelley, in his 1972 book, *Why Conservative Churches Are Growing*, attributed that difference to the conservative theology and evangelistic commitment promoted by evangelicals. However, in more recent decades, it appears that many of America's conservative congregations and many of its dynamic megachurches have stopped growing. The Christian Reformed Church peaked in 1992,[44] the Southern Baptist Convention peaked in 2006,[45] the Evangelical Presbyterian Church peaked in 2016,[46] and attendance at Willow Creek Community Church in Illinois peaked in 2015 and is now a third of what it once was.[47] Forces are clearly at work within North American society that negatively impact congregations across the theological spectrum. No wonder there is now a widespread feeling of defeat across most denominations, and a dread that the North American church will collapse.

With that, I return to Willow Creek Community Church, whose founding pastor Bill Hybels left in 2016, accused of sexual impropriety. Scot McKnight wrote a critique of Hybels and Willow Creek in 2019, calling the congregation "probably the most influential evangelical church in the world." He writes that Hybels "reshaped the job description, image and toolbox of what pastoring is understood to be," drew leaders from across the globe to see how seeker-sensitive church should be done, and built an organizational brand name that remained after his departure.[48] To examine the job description developed by Willow Creek to guide its search for Hybels's

43. Webster, *Selling Jesus*, 66.
44. Christian Reformed Church, "Yearbook and Online Data."
45. Shellnutt, "SBC Membership Falls."
46. Kincaid, "EPC Continues to Grow."
47. Perry, "Willow Creek and Harvest."
48. McKnight, "Willow Creek's Troubles."

successor, McKnight pasted it to a word cloud app and discovered that the word "Willow" dominated: management of the Willow Creek brand defined the pastoral position, not the biblical categories one would expect, says McKnight. The job description's terms are not likely to be found "in any word cloud about Jesus' pastoral life or Peter's pastoral life, or Paul's."[49] McKnight concludes that the Willow Creek entrepreneurial leadership model—though it undoubtedly offered new vitality to thousands of congregational leaders seeking solutions for their troubled congregations—overrides New Testament teaching on what shapes pastoral leadership, which is, he says, to nurture Christoformity.

Critical of the entrepreneurial leadership promoted by congregations like Willow Creek, Robert Osborne, a Canadian spiritual director, wrote a fascinating paper in 2005 titled "Spiritual Leadership as Representative." "It appears more and more," he writes, "that current leadership language is merely a further entrenchment of the values of efficiency and productivity that inspire our business culture."[50] But, says Osborne, pastoral ministry can't be reduced to technique, speed, process, cost, and efficiency, for life "is extravagant, wasteful, slow, relational." He goes on to suggest what spiritual leadership is by examining the Acts 1 story of how the first Christians waited for Pentecost:

> In obedience to Christ's word of promise they waited for the blessing of the Spirit, and in waiting ... they prayed (Acts 1:14) and they settled their leadership questions (Acts 1:23), and each informed the other. They did not choose leaders apart from the practice of their spirituality [prayer], and the leaders they chose were persons of spiritual practice [being followers of Jesus] .... Leadership in the early Christian community wasn't selected to do organizational work *per se*, but to do the work of witness and prayer.[51]

In looking at how Jesus's disciples replaced Judas, Osborne notes that the key qualification for the potential new leader was that they had followed Jesus from the start of his ministry to his resurrection (Acts 1:21); faithful witness was required, not self-initiating creativity. Osborne says that while "Current leadership literature uses the human record of achievement to explain what it is that leaders do .... Spiritual leadership is not about coming up with a new self-initiated vision. It is about seeing, living in, and

---

49. McKnight, "Willow Creek's Troubles."
50. Osborne, "Spiritual Leadership," 1–2.
51. Osborne, "Spiritual Leadership," 2–3.

announcing [what] God has already started . . . a story that is bigger than any of us."[52] In contrast to "an uncritical openness to secular, nonbiblical paradigms of leadership," Osborne sees church leadership as "the yielding of will to the purpose of God, the call to be a servant of divine purpose, to become the least, to follow in the way of Jesus."[53]

Osborne respects New Testament thinking. He contrasts the ministry of Jesus and his first disciples with the ministry of current church leaders who are too impressed by the success stories of Peter Drucker or Steve Covey, and who are overly ready to transfer strategies to congregations borrowed from the world of commerce. This transference, however, does not necessarily respect the unique identity of congregations as God-created communities that find their life, energy, and purpose in Christ, or as Jesus put it, who, like the branches of a vine, are to abide in him (John 15:1-5).

Yet perhaps Osborne goes too far in the other direction. He rightly notes the prayerful, spiritual discernment of church leaders in Acts 1, but does not seem to take into account how, later in Acts, those leaders used common sense to delegate to others the task of food distribution in Jerusalem (Acts 6), strategically preached Jesus in synagogues where the Old Testament was already known (Acts 13:13-43), and organized a council to discuss how to include gentiles within the church (Acts 15) or how the apostle Paul cleverly took advantage of his Roman citizenship to avoid a flogging by Roman authorities (Acts 22). Yes, leaders must discern and respect a congregation's identity as God's *ekklesia*, but that does not preclude the use of skills and strategies retrieved from the world at large. That said, I thoroughly agree with Osborne that, enthralled by technique, congregational leaders are tempted to bypass the essence of spiritual leadership. Craig Van Gelder clarifies the point: "The church is more than meets the eye. It is more than a set of well-managed ministry functions. It is more than another human organization. The church lives in the world as a human enterprise, but it is also the called and redeemed people of God. . . . As such, the church is both a social organization and a spiritual community."[54]

As previously stated, respect for a congregation means taking time to understand that it is both a social organization and a spiritual community, a double identity that challenges not only congregations but those who study them. Widely used in seminaries, the 1998 book *Studying Congregations*,

---

52. Osborne, "Spiritual Leadership," 5.
53. Osborne, "Spiritual Leadership," 2.
54. Van Gelder, *Essence of the Church*, 116.

The Challenge Involved in Respecting Congregations

written by America's leading congregational researchers, Nancy T. Ammerman, Jackson W. Carroll, Carl S. Dudley, and William McKinney, gives students and church leaders a wide range of tools with which to analyze a congregation. Respectful of the wisdom of lay people as well as that of clergy, *Studying Congregations* affirms the uniqueness of each congregation's context, history, culture, resources, and internal processes.

Studying Congregations is a most valuable tool for understanding congregations, but it is also limited. Other than a few references to seeking God's purposes, particularly in Jackson Carroll's chapter, the book is relentlessly horizontal and sociological in its approach to the congregations that dot the North American landscape. As to why those congregations should exist or why new ones should be built, no answer is given, and though the book has a chapter on theology, theology seems to be understood in *Studying Congregations* as the uncovering of the religious values held by the members of any given congregation. Otherwise, the book eschews the New Testament narration of the life, death, and resurrection of Jesus; the coming of the Spirit; and the resulting emergence of God's *ekklesia*. In his introduction to *Missional Church*, published in 1998, Darrell Guder indicts this sort of approach to congregations in these words:

> We do not believe ... that once the sociologist or historian describes a particular church as a fully human, thoroughly sociological organism, there is nothing more to say of it. While the church is always a real, human, social organism, it is also the body of Christ, a community grafted into the life of God in its baptism and by the action of the Holy Spirit. Elements of it are true that are not made visible by the categories and presuppositions of the sociologist, elements that rest deep in its faith and hope in the divine promises.[55]

Helpful yet equally limited is some of the popular material produced to help North America's congregations to rediscover their purpose. Take New Beginnings, a program of Hope Partnership Services promoted by my denomination, the Presbyterian Church in Canada. New Beginnings helps congregations to seek a new direction by entering what the Presbyterian Church in Canada's website describes as a "yearlong transformational process of spiritual discernment" that will help congregations "looking to discern God's call for their future and create a plan to move forward."[56] The process begins with a Hope Assessor being appointed to a congregation. The

---

55. Guder, "Missional Church," 12–13.
56. Presbyterian Church in Canada, "New Beginnings."

assessor is to evaluate all statistical data gathered by the congregation; visit the congregation to interact with and gather stories from congregants; write a report that reviews the congregation's demographics, finances, buildings, ministries; and offer three possible future directions for the congregation. At that point, a denominationally appointed guide helps the congregation to complete the process: the guide trains facilitators to lead small groups to reflect on the assessor's report, to elicit responses from those groups, and to ensure that the congregation ends up with a way forward.

I appreciate the thoroughness of the New Beginnings process and the likelihood that it will help congregations toward a new future; an insightful assessor and guide can offer a congregation a good deal of fresh self-understanding. But though much about New Beginnings is valuable, the process assumes that congregational members who meet to talk, share, and pray around tables will reach consensus about what God wants for the congregation's future. It is good that New Beginnings gives time and space for congregants to air their values, dreams, and desires, but it must be said that its use of well-known elements of the democratic process will not necessarily capture what the New Testament says about a congregation's identity, purpose, and ministry.

Strangely, not once does the five-page outline of the New Beginnings process mention Jesus, the Lord whom Christians confess and the foundation on which their congregations are built. While New Beginnings certainly urges prayer for discernment, it is not explicitly Christian. And while New Beginnings respects the importance of a congregation's local identity, it appears to bypass what I stress—that a congregation is a Spirit-led, "in Christ" community sent into the world to witness to Christ. It may be that New Beginnings expects assessors, coaches, and congregants to bring rich, biblical insights to the conversation about congregational identity and purpose, but not to even allude to such is disheartening.

For a congregation to discover clarity of purpose, it should, of course, consider its context, culture, values, dreams, and desires, all of which New Beginnings encourages. But at the same time, it should examine its context, culture, values, dreams, and desires in the light of God's word, which judges what is by what ought to be. Admittedly, it is hard to grasp all that the New Testament says about congregational identity and purpose, but to bypass that hard work disrespects congregations.

The Challenge Involved in Respecting Congregations

NOW WHAT?

I suggest that current congregations find it hard to respect the identity, purpose, and ministry priorities that the New Testament proposes for at least three reasons. A first reason is the reluctance to let go of the idea that congregations can solve their own problems. In *Joining God, Remaking Church, Changing the World*, Alan Roxburgh writes that churches have "an overriding conviction that with the right techniques and methods it is possible to usher in the kingdom. This belief system runs in the background of all the surveys to determine how healthy your church is, all the reorganizational strategies, all the techniques for how to grow a church."[57] Such fixing methods will not work, he says, because they are "based on the assumption that the only thing necessary is some adjustment," and that God will somehow function "as a background resource to support our own management efforts."[58] Congregations must dare to ask who is finally in charge.

A second reason today's congregations find it hard to take New Testament approaches to congregations seriously is the distance between what the New Testament says about leadership and what constitutes good leadership in our current culture. Earlier I noted the concerns raised by Eugene Peterson, Robert Osborne, and others, about the entrepreneurial leadership now promoted within North American congregations. Successful leadership in such circles is often measured by attendance and, in some cases, by how many new campuses a congregation has planted. Congregational leaders who have been or are still held up as models of success include Bill Hybels, Bill Easum, Rick Warren, T. D. Jakes, Andy Stanley, Rob Bell, Mark Driscoll, and Joel Osteen, male leaders of mostly nondenominational congregations. But recall my chapter 2 discussion of how the apostle Paul responded to the championing of various leaders within Corinth's congregation: "What then is Apollos? What is Paul? Servants through whom you came to believe, as the Lord assigned to each" (1 Cor 3:5).

The Bible says much more about costly service than successful leadership, a key topic in current congregational leadership material. In their 2020 book, *A Church Called Tov*, Scot McKnight and Laura Barringer vigorously challenge the current fascination with leaders and leadership in American congregations: "Do you know how many times Jesus talked about people becoming leaders? Not once .... Yes, pastors provide some

---

57. Roxburgh, *Joining God, Remaking Church*, 26.
58. Roxburgh, *Joining God, Remaking Church*, 31.

leadership, but they should be leading toward spiritual formation," for congregational life is about "a community of believers and being nurtured in the faith . . . about soul work and confession of sin . . . about relationship and community . . . about knowing and being known, loving and being loved, serving and being served."[59] That description respects what a congregation is and what a congregation does as a local family of God that is being redeemed and restored. It also respects the servant nature of congregational leadership. As Paul wrote in 2 Cor 4:5, "we do not proclaim ourselves; we proclaim Jesus Christ as Lord and ourselves as your slaves for Jesus' sake." What does that mean? Leadership "for Jesus' sake" means that before leaders lead a congregation, while leaders lead a congregation, and after leaders lead a congregation, they will submit as servants to Jesus. But what congregations of all sizes want are not submissive servants but heroic leaders. Here again, Eugene Peterson offers insight: "One of the first things that strikes us about the men and women in Scripture is that they were disappointingly nonheroic. We do not find splendid moral examples. We do not find impeccably virtuous models . . . Abraham lied; Jacob cheated; Moses murdered and complained; David committed adultery; Peter blasphemed."[60] Peterson reminds us that, as Martin Luther put it, we are *simul justus et peccator*—righteous before God through faith in Jesus, but at the same time, flawed sinners who need forgiveness.

The apostle Paul, founder of Corinth's congregation, did not present himself as a hero. To the contrary, he told the congregation that he was "unfit to be called an apostle" because he had persecuted the church (1 Cor 15:9). His message to that congregation, as I discussed in chapter 2, was essentially this: "It was Christ who died *for* you, not me; it is *through* Christ's death, not mine, that God forgave you; it is *on* Christ, not me, that your congregation is being built; it is *in* Christ, risen and reigning, not me, that you find God's life and power." Ah!

A third reason today's congregations find it hard to respect what the New Testament says about congregational identity, purpose, and ministry priorities is that they have not been in the habit of going to the New Testament to discover such things. Christians may look to the Bible for direction or inspiration, but looking to the New Testament to discover what a congregation is or why it exists is rare in current congregational literature. Efforts to reverse the decline of North America's congregations focus on a

---

59. McKnight and Barringer, *Church Called Tov*, 214–15.
60. Peterson, *Run with the Horses*, 12.

The Challenge Involved in Respecting Congregations

range of strategies—seven-day-a-week congregations; attractional congregations; small group ministry congregations; evangelistically targeted congregations; regional rather than local congregations; emotionally healthy congregations; and, post-COVID, the possibility of replacing physical congregations in part or in whole with online congregations. Such functionalist strategies treat congregations as organizations, but beyond a congregation's organizational identity lies the unexplored New Testament material that offers a theological identity and missional purpose to congregations. Seemingly, Lyle Schaller's untheological approach to congregations lives on!

What does the future hold for our congregations? For centuries, congregations assumed their existence, a mindset that, still in place in the 1950s, encouraged the building of thousands of suburban congregations in North America that never supposed they would one day unravel. Now, some one hundred congregations close every week across North America. So, is the church in the West in the process of disappearing? That is unlikely, if for no other reason than that Christianity is growing in Africa, South Asia, and Latin America; additionally, from such places, ardent believers emigrate to North America, some of them as missionaries. Philip Jenkins's 2002 book, *The Next Christendom: The Coming of Global Christianity*, describes this phenomenon and alerts Western Christians to the fact that Christianity's center of gravity is no longer Europe or North America, but the Global South. There, despite poverty, political corruption, a shortage of clergy, and threats of persecution, congregations keep multiplying, unlike in North America.[61] Jenkins, challenging the assumption that Christianity is in decline, explains how Christians in the Global South read the Bible in ways alien to Christians in North America:

> Southern churches are quite at home with biblical notions of the supernatural ... for the average Western audience, New Testament passages about standing firm in the face of pagan persecution have little immediate relevance.... But for millions of Southern Christians ... they might someday find themselves before a tribunal that would demand that they renounce their faith upon pain of death.... In this context, the book of Revelation looks like true prophecy on an epic scale, however unpopular or discredited it may be for most Americans or Europeans. In the South, Revelation simply makes sense, in its description of a world ruled by monstrous demonic powers.[62]

---

61. See Jenkins, *Next Christendom*, 244–49.
62. Jenkins, *Next Christendom*, 257–59.

North American congregations living in an affluent, advanced technological society read the Bible differently. Though those congregations acknowledge God's presence and power, they tend to look elsewhere for help to fix themselves. Alan Roxburgh writes, "Ours is a world of calculation, control, and predictability. A conviction of God's agency in the world is displaced with actions empty of any sense of God's working."[63] In other words, God is held at a distance by congregations who trust themselves rather than read and respect New Testament teaching about God's plans and purposes for congregations.

CONCLUSION

In the rush to retool congregations for the twenty-first century, a good deal of disrespect is perpetrated. The wisdom of the past is discounted; the temptation to play one generation off against another is approved; demands for change cause clergy to connect with one segment of a congregation and ignore a less responsive segment; congregations are subject to unending visions, revisions, and reconstructions. How ought we to respond to this? The answer, I suggest, is neither to be more civil nor to avoid conflict, though these tactics have more to commend them than some imagine! What is key is to see a congregation as God sees it, and to respect that though a congregation is a social organization, it is primarily a spiritual community connected to the ultimate reality for which we pray, the coming of the kingdom of God.

I end this chapter by reflecting on Karl Barth, likely the twentieth century's most important Protestant theologian. I do so because Barth paid attention to the church and to congregations. I note with pleasure Barth's awareness that congregations have both "in Corinth" and "in Christ" identities. In volume IV/2 of his *Church Dogmatics*, he writes that, subject to all kinds of pressures under which it may stumble and fall, "the church is . . . a human, earthly-historical-construct, whose history involves from the very first, and always will involve, human action."[64] Yet, writes Barth, in God's *ekklesia*, that is, in congregations,

> The crucified Jesus Christ lives . . . . And this means that, although He lives also and primarily as the exalted Son of Man, at the right hand of the Father . . . He does not live only there but lives too . . . in the little communities in Thessalonica and Corinth and

---

63. Roxburgh, *Joining God, Remaking Church*, 30.
64. Barth, *Church Dogmatics*, IV/2:616.

> Philippi, in Galatia and at Rome . . . . As we are told in Jn.15:4f, they have no being or life apart from Him, just as the branches are nothing apart from the vine.[65]

Barth admits that, facing various "in Corinth" issues, there will be times "when the witness that [the church] ought to give is either omitted or obscured and falsified; when the pride or sloth of man, or both together, is what is expressed and revealed."[66] Yet, like Paul, Barth holds that, despite its failures, the *ekklesia* as an "in Christ" body has within it a power beyond itself, namely, "Jesus the Lord who is at work in this quickening power of the Holy Spirit."[67]

I also note how Barth's personal history alerts us to the importance of respecting the place of Jesus in the church and congregations. Barth gained prominence after publishing a commentary on Paul's Letter to the Romans in 1919. Here is how my friend John Vissers describes its impact:

> Karl Barth's book was an astonishingly brash challenge to the hegemony of nineteenth-century liberal theology . . . . The second edition, published in 1922, erupted with even more volcanic power as Barth pointed to the centrality of the Word of God which touched time and history in Jesus Christ, and which continues to touch humanity again and again as the original word is heard . . . . Religion, Barth argued, far from being the point of closest contact with God, is the house human beings made in order to hide themselves from God, to convince themselves that God is within their grasp and under their control . . . . The cross of Jesus Christ is God's final and decisive "No!" to all that: it leaves us literally nothing of our own on which we can rely.[68]

Barth learned what can happen if the church fails to give Jesus a central place, when in 1933 Hitler's Nazi Party assumed power in Germany. Appalled by how many German Protestant congregations accepted Nazi ideology and remained silent as Hitler challenged the church's Christian identity, Barth and others responded by issuing The Barmen Declaration in 1934. It stated that "Jesus Christ, as he is attested for us in Holy Scripture, is the one Word of God which we have to hear and which we have to trust and obey in life and in death. We reject the false doctrine, as though the

---

65. Barth, *Church Dogmatics*, IV/2:658–59.
66. Barth, *Church Dogmatics*, IV/2:617–18.
67. Barth, *Church Dogmatics*, IV/2:651.
68. Vissers, *Neo-Orthodox Theology of W. W. Bryden*, 3–4.

church could and would have to acknowledge as a source of its proclamation, apart from and besides this one Word of God, still other events and powers, figures and truths, as God's revelation."[69]

Barth's insistence on the central place of Jesus Christ in the church remains a live issue for North American Christians. I say this conscious that some mainline congregations, seeking to be inclusive, reduce references to Jesus and refer instead to God, Spirit, and even Mother Earth. Then there are those congregations caught up in the Trumpian notion that Jesus can be co-opted to endorse the MAGA movement. In *Church Dogmatics* IV/2, written a decade after Hitler died, Barth says what North American congregations need to hear: "The voice which has to be heard is that of Jesus Christ as attested in Holy Scripture. It is in the form attested there that He is the Head, the living Lord of the community."[70]

I also end this chapter with Barth to anticipate the discussion in chapter 4 of the purpose of congregations. As stated earlier, theologians do not always give congregations serious theological attention; for their part, congregations often think of theologians as irrelevant ivory-tower theorists. The result: Congregations remain unaware of how theology might help them to faithfully live out their vocation. Instead, time and energy have been spent in recent decades on strategies to stimulate congregational growth—use new Bible translations; try up-to-date technology; get rid of hymnbooks; make worship seeker-sensitive; tighten up on church discipline, now in vogue in the Irish Presbyterian Church of my youth; or loosen up on church discipline, now in vogue in the Canadian Presbyterian Church. Much less time and energy have gone to working out a Bible-based theology of congregations that respects their role in God's mission. That situation is now changing, in large part because of Karl Barth.

So, I turn with pleasure to a group of North American theologians whose aim isn't only to clarify the theological significance of congregations but to help congregations be communities of God that serve God's mission. I refer to the Gospel and Our Culture Network (GOCN), begun in the late 1980s. The GOCN's leaders, including Craig Van Gelder, Darrell Guder, and George Hunsberger, were inspired by British theologian Lesslie Newbigin, who in turn was inspired by none other than Karl Barth! Their theological work, I am convinced, offers North American congregations the sort of respect that will help them to thrive.

---

69. Quoted in *Our Confessional Heritage*, 154.
70. Barth, *Church Dogmatics*, IV/2:682–83.

4

Theological Respect for Congregations

CHAPTER 1 INTRODUCED THE idea of respecting congregations, which may have merely seemed like a call for congregations to behave with greater civility. But of course, the real focus of my book is respect *for* congregations. On the meaning of respect, recall philosopher Robin Dillon's words that define respect as "a form of regard: a mode of attention to and acknowledgment of an object as something to be taken seriously. Respecting something contrasts with being oblivious or indifferent to it, ignoring or quickly dismissing it, neglecting or disregarding it, or carelessly or intentionally misidentifying it."[1] Chapter 2 then articulated how the New Testament attends to and carefully nurtures congregational identity and purpose. Chapter 3 pointed out, however, that North American congregations find it hard to recognize let alone respect their identity and purpose, one reason being that believers reading "you" in Paul's letters assume that it refers to an individual, not a congregation, which leaves congregations unaware of how much the New Testament says to and about them.

As discussed in chapter 3, North America's congregations have numerically declined since the 1960s, an ongoing process that causes them to turn inward to try to diagnose and fix their problems. Though the numerical decline of evangelical congregations came later than the decline of mainline congregations, I suspect that fears about congregational futures

---

1. Dillon, "Respect," §1.1.

haunts all of them. If I am correct, the big question is this: What are congregations for, beyond sustaining themselves? To answer that question, I turn to the missional theologians who say that we respect congregations when we understand not only their theological identity but also their missional purpose in relation to God's plan to reestablish God's rule and restore God's whole creation.

INTRODUCING NORTH AMERICA'S MISSIONAL THEOLOGIANS

In 2001, I taught a seminary congregational leadership course for the first time. It may have interested students preparing to be pastors, but it did not theologically engage them. The reason is this: I taught from my experience of congregational leadership and used as a core text *Studying Congregations*, referred to in chapter 3 as offering functional and organizational insights to congregations but not theological ones. Revising the course for the next academic year, I read *The Essence of the Church* by missional theologian Craig Van Gelder. He values organizational approaches to congregations but argues that congregations must also see themselves as linked theologically to God's kingdom and God's mission. However, I had for years relied on practical strategies to help congregations, largely unaware of how theological reflection on congregational identity and purpose can help them.

As stated earlier, twentieth-century theology did not give significant theological attention to congregations, in part because academic theology does not always prioritize the doctrine of the church. In fact, during the Enlightenment, particularly in Germany, a concerted effort was made to move the study of theology from church institutions to more intellectually rigorous universities, where it could be studied free of ecclesiastical oversight. It was this liberal, nonconfessional, church-suspicious theology to which Karl Barth reacted after the First World War. For Barth and his disciples, theology is about how the church reflects on the Christian faith for the sake of the church, an approach that gained traction during the twentieth century and that would eventually encourage theological reflection on congregations.

The missional theologians I now introduce, inspired by the British missionary theologian Lesslie Newbigin, formed the Gospel and Our Culture Network (GOCN) in the late 1980s. At the end of the twentieth century, the GOCN, including Darrell Guder, Lois Barrett, Inagrace Dietterich, George

Theological Respect for Congregations

Hunsberger, Alan Roxburgh, and Craig Van Gelder, read the Bible seeking a fresh vision for the North American church, by then experiencing precipitous numerical decline. Having examined New Testament thinking about the church and its congregations, which I tried to summarize in chapter 2, the GOCN reframed their understanding of the church's identity and purpose in relation to three theological themes: the kingdom of God, the trinitarian nature of God, and the mission of God. Thankfully, they included a respect for congregations, which they chose to call "missional communities."

This theological attentiveness to congregations parallels the theological attentiveness in Andrew Purves's book *Reconstructing Pastoral Theology*. Purves complains that American mainline seminaries organize pastoral theology around a psychological interpretation of human experience, use psychotherapeutic categories alien to those of the Bible and Christian doctrine, and promote pastoral care that aims at self-actualization rather than salvation. Purves does not dismiss insights from psychology, yet argues that the foundation for pastoral theology rests on God's ministry enacted by Jesus, whom God sent for our healing, forgiveness, and salvation: "Pastoral theology, then, before it is a theology of what the church or the pastor does, is . . . a theology of the pastoring God."[2] Classic doctrines, writes Purves—whether God's triune nature or Christ's incarnation, atonement, resurrection, and ascension—answer the perennial problems that humans face. To illustrate, he notes that "the love that flows between the Father and the Son in the unity of the Holy Spirit reveals that God is a God of love within the communion of the Holy Trinity," reassuring us that God will always love us, and that there is "no secret God lurking behind the facade of God's love in Jesus Christ, ready to judge us with law rather than love."[3]

I take note of Purves because I believe that his theological approach to pastoral care needs to be paralleled by a theological approach to congregations, which is exactly what the GOCN theologians offer. The core message of their 1998 collection of essays titled *Missional Church*, edited by Darrell Guder, is this: Just as God the Father sent the Son, and just as the Father and the Son sent the Spirit, so God, Father, Son, and Spirit, send the church to be a tangible sign, agent, and foretaste of the inaugurated but not yet fully established kingdom of God. In this view, congregations are meant to be concrete, credible embodiments of the rule or kingdom of God that

---

2. Purves, *Reconstructing Pastoral Theology*, 4.
3. Purves, *Reconstructing Pastoral Theology*, 36–37.

Jesus inaugurated. I will liberally quote from *Missional Church* to capture its respect for congregations as God's people sent on a mission.

FIRST, GOD'S KINGDOM

Before discussing what the GOCN theologians say about congregations, I reflect on the watchword that defined Jesus's ministry, and one that lies at the core of missional theology: the kingdom of God. By the end of the twentieth century, most theologians were agreed that the kingdom of God was central to Jesus's message, even if not all agreed on what he meant by it. Catholic and Protestant exegetes traditionally identified the kingdom of God with the church; thus, the Victorian divine Richard Trench wrote in his *Notes on the Parables of Our Lord* that Jesus's parables that compare God's kingdom to a tiny mustard seed and leaven "describe the small and slight beginnings, the gradual progress, and the final marvelous increase of the Church."[4] However, at the end of the nineteenth century, liberal German theologians like Adolf von Harnack distanced God's kingdom from the church. Stephen Neill sums up Harnack's theological priorities as the coming of God's kingdom, the Father and the infinite value of the human soul, and the higher righteousness and the commandment of love. Harnack, writes Neill, thought of the kingdom as a growing, spiritually enlightened society, with Jesus as "its personal realization and its strength."[5]

Prior to the First World War, the idea of the kingdom as a Jesus-inspired, progressive, ideal society was popularized in America by preachers like Nevell Dwight Hillis. He enthused about the kingdom in these words, "Laws are becoming more just, rulers more humane; music is becoming sweeter and books wiser; homes are happier, and the individual heart is becoming once just and more gentle . . . for today, art, industry, invention, literature, learning, and government—all these are captives marching in Christ's triumphant procession."[6] This "belief in the early and relatively painless realization of the kingdom of God on earth,"[7] wrote the Canadian church historian John Webster Grant, fueled the formation of the United Church of Canada in 1925 by Congregationalists, Methodists, and most but not all Presbyterians.

4. Trench, *Notes on the Parables*, 91.
5. Neill, *Interpretation of the New Testament*, 134–35.
6. Quoted in Fosdick, *Living of These Days*, 237.
7. Grant, *Canadian Experience of Church Union*, 32.

Theological Respect for Congregations

In his book *Sign of the Kingdom*, Lesslie Newbigin claims that Protestant liberals embraced the kingdom as "wider, more inclusive, less sectarian than the message of salvation through Jesus Christ";[8] he quotes the 1932 Laymen's Enquiry into Foreign Missions' Report that said that the aim of Christian mission was to contribute to "social progress" and "the communication of spiritual values." Seeing the kingdom as "something very much broader than can be defined by allegiance to the Person of Jesus," says Newbigin, "meant that preaching, evangelism, conversion, baptism and the building up of the Church became relatively peripheral concerns."[9] In the 1960s, theological radicals urged that the idea of God blessing the world through the church should be abandoned because "it is the world which writes the agenda for the Church."[10]

As to what Jesus meant by the kingdom of God, three views dominate, all of which contain elements of the truth: (1) the kingdom is a Jesus-inspired vision of a new social order, (2) the kingdom will in apocalyptic style end the present dispensation and usher in a new one, and (3) the kingdom is the rule of Christ now at work in the church that will one day be universal. This last view, on which the GOCN builds, was developed by biblical scholars who subjected to exegetical scrutiny the loose ways in which kingdom language was often used during the twentieth century. Typical of that scrutiny is R. T. France's 1990 book, *Divine Government*, where he, a cautious British Anglican, exegetes the "kingdom of God" phrase in Mark's Gospel and clarifies at least five critical issues.

First, Jesus's announcement, "The time is fulfilled, and the kingdom of God has come near; repent and believe in the good news" (Mark 1:14). France states that the New Testament rarely, and Mark's Gospel never, refers to the "kingdom," but to the full phrase "kingdom of God." The reason, he says, is that the word kingdom doesn't refer to a physical territory but to the fact of God's rule; accordingly, the kingdom "is a statement about God . . . *God* in control, *God* working out his purpose." Thus, talk about the kingdom "is about as meaningless as to talk about 'the will' or 'the power' without a reference to whose will or power is in view."[11] France's exegetical point undermines those who attempt to distance or even separate the kingdom from God's person.

---

8. Newbigin, *Sign of the Kingdom*, vii.
9. Newbigin, *Sign of the Kingdom*, 6–7.
10. Newbigin, *Sign of the Kingdom*, 13.
11. France, *Divine Government*, 13.

Second, France notes the verbs that Mark's Gospel associates with the kingdom of God. Instead of talking of building, growing, extending, or establishing God's kingdom, Mark's Gospel talks of those who "wait," "welcome," "enter," or "receive" God's kingdom.[12] This insight challenges the idea that the kingdom is something achieved by human progress and clarifies that God's kingdom is in God's control and is God's gift to be received by repentance and faith. Craig Van Gelder makes the same point: "The basic idea of the kingdom is that God in Jesus powerfully entered human history with a reign that . . . is about the dynamic presence of God's redemptive power confronting the forces of evil and restoring life to its fullness."[13]

Third, France notes that Old Testament references to the kingdom of God are rare but that the idea of God as king is not. In particular, he refers to kingship language in the book of Daniel that predicts "the replacement of all human empires by the one unshakeable kingdom," and how one "like a son of man" will establish "an everlasting dominion that shall not pass away, and his kingship is one that shall never be destroyed" (Dan 7:14).[14] Noting that in Mark's Gospel Jesus refers to himself as the Son of Man, France links that figure to the coming kingdom of God (Mark 8:38—9:1) and quotes the conclusion of Chrys Caragounis that "the Son of Man and the Kingdom of God are in Jesus' teaching indissolubly connected."[15] While Jesus's Jewish audience would have heard his announcement of God's kingdom as echoing their hope that God would release Israel from its oppressors, that audience would have been confused by Jesus's talk of God's kingdom, not as a dramatic change of government, but as God taking over, bringing both salvation and judgment, and the Son of Man becoming a victim of nationalist violence, not the winner of a nationalist victory. France insists that Jesus's understanding of the kingdom of God must be read against a Jewish background, something that Western liberals often ignore.

Fourth, as to whether God's kingdom is future or imminent, France argues that the perfect tense verb *engiken*, translated in Mark 1:15 as "the kingdom of God has come near," refers to the imminent arrival of something long expected. But while Jesus announced the imminent arrival of God's kingdom, the Gospels go on to teach that it has yet to be fully realized. The kingdom, writes France, "both 'has come' and 'is coming,' just

---

12. France, *Divine Government*, 14.
13. Van Gelder, *Essence of the Church*, 75.
14. France, *Divine Government*, 17–18.
15. France, *Divine Government*, 18.

Theological Respect for Congregations

as in the longer version of the Lord's Prayer we balance 'Your kingdom come' with 'Yours is the kingdom.'" Thus Mark 1:15 does not offer a precise timescale, says France; its point is "that it is *in the coming of Jesus* that we are to see God's revolution taking place. Indeed, it is *in Jesus* that we are to see God coming as king."[16]

The identification of Jesus as king of God's kingdom is critical for Lesslie Newbigin and the GOCN theologians. Tired of the idea reiterated during the twentieth century that the kingdom of God is an ideology, program, or campaign that Christians are to implement to produce a better world, Newbigin states in *Sign of the Kingdom* that the good news Jesus announced—"the kingdom of God has come near"—is that Jesus is king of the kingdom. I quote:

> Why . . . was the liberal Christianity of the 1920s so eager to separate the Kingdom of God from the name of Jesus? . . . eager to talk about the coming of the kingdom but so very reluctant to speak of the second coming of Jesus? . . . ready with the prayer "Thy Kingdom come" but so reluctant to pray "Come, Lord Jesus"? . . . Jesus did indeed preach the kingdom, but the only thing that made his preaching news was that the kingdom was present in himself . . . . The news is that "the kingdom of God" is no longer merely a theological phrase. There is now a name and a human face.[17]

Fifth, convinced that Jesus's arrival meant the arrival of God's kingdom, France suggests that Mark's Gospel fills out what Jesus meant by the kingdom. Yet what Jesus said about God's kingdom, though it attracted Jewish nationalists, must also have disappointed them, for it endorsed neither the violent coup hoped for by Jewish zealots nor the robust law and order regime hoped for by the Pharisees; rather, Jesus announced, "many who are first will be last, and the last will be first" (Mark 10:31), a verse, says France, that points to a subversive kingdom whose king "came not to be served but to serve" (Mark 10:45). Far from being "the sort of revolution many of Jesus' hearers were looking for,"[18] writes France, Mark's Gospel portrays the kingdom of God as a confrontation between Jesus and evil forces (Mark 1:24–27, 5:1–13, 9:17–27).

France's exegesis of the kingdom of God in Mark's Gospel aligns with that of Britain's better known biblical exegete, N. T. Wright. Like France,

---

16. France, *Divine Government*, 24–25. Italics original.
17. Newbigin, *Sign of the Kingdom*, 32–33.
18. France, *Divine Government*, 47.

Wright integrates the message of Jesus about God's kingdom, narrated in the Gospels, with Jesus's person. While most theologians agree that the kingdom of God was a major theme in Jesus's teaching, not all see him as that kingdom's king. Wright emphatically does. Like France, he sees the book of Daniel as key to Jesus's conviction that God had sent him to set up what Dan 7:14 describes as "an everlasting dominion that shall not pass away." Not only did Jesus relate the arrival of this promised dominion or kingdom directly to himself, but "he and those who later told his story linked it directly and dynamically to his own death"—a death, says Wright, anticipated in the words of Dan 9:24 that describe a time when God plans "to finish the transgression, to put an end to sin, to atone for iniquity, and thereby to win the ultimate victory over the powers of evil."[19]

Wright also integrates Jesus's kingdom emphasis with the apostle Paul's emphasis on Jesus's death and resurrection. Quoting Paul's words in 1 Cor 15:4 ("I handed on to you as of first importance what I had in turn received: that Christ died for our sins in accordance with the scriptures, and that he was buried, and that he was raised on the third day in accordance with the scriptures"), Wright explains that by writing that Jesus's death and resurrection happened "in accordance with the scriptures," Paul places Jesus within the Bible's overarching story of God reestablishing his kingdom, not by force but through a suffering servant. Wright comments: "Jesus of Nazareth went to his death believing that this would be the ultimate good news moment.... As the four Gospels indicate, it comes down ... to a battle between Jesus, as the pioneer of God's kingdom on earth as in heaven, and the accuser, the satan, the dark quasi-personal force bent on destroying God's work, God's kingdom, God's world ... [and] God's son." Wright adds,

> What looked like a judicial punishment meted out upon Jesus was ... meted out *upon evil itself*.... Therefore sinners who are now "in the Messiah" can be confident that there is "no condemnation" for them.... This is why the kingdom of God, which Jesus had launched in his public career, was inaugurated in a whole new way with his death and resurrection. What was holding back the kingdom was the dark power, the force of evil itself. On the cross, that force, that power was defeated.[20]

Wright emphasizes that the good news Paul received and passed on (1 Cor 15:1) included not only Jesus's death but his resurrection. For Paul,

---

19. Wright, *Day the Revolution Began*, 119.
20. Wright, *Simply Good News*, 44–45. Italics original.

the resurrection was not primarily about proving that there is life after death or that people go to heaven when they die; rather, says Wright, the resurrection meant that all authority in heaven and on earth has now been given to Jesus, king of the kingdom: "The good news is that *the one true God has now taken charge of the world, in and through Jesus and his death and resurrection* . . . . The ancient sickness that had crippled the whole world, and humans with it, has been cured at last, so that new life can rise up in its place." The good news, says Wright, is that "all this *has* happened in and through Jesus [and] that one day it *will* happen, completely and utterly, to all creation; *and that we humans, every single one of us, whoever we are, can be caught up in that transformation here and now.*"[21]

For Wright, the kingdom isn't a Jesus-inspired human project, but God reestablishing his rule over a rebellious world through Jesus's life, death, and resurrection. Scot McKnight makes the same point in his book *Kingdom Conspiracy* by reflecting on three of Jesus's titles in the Gospels—Son of Man, Son of God, and Messiah. He notes that all three, when carefully exegeted, refer to a ruler who suffers; each title, says McKnight, "tells the story of Jesus as one who was sent by God to bring fulfillment to Israel's story by reclaiming the rule of God in this world. Each tells the story of Jesus's full life: he was born of a virgin, lived a very Jewish life, declared the kingdom with himself at the center, formed a group of followers, died both as a victim of injustice and as an act of God to end injustice by dying the death of others, and was raised to the right hand of the Father to rule."[22]

Echoing McKnight, George Hunsberger's chapter in *Missional Church* sums up the gospel of the kingdom in these words: "Ruling by way of a cross and a resurrection, God thwarts the powers of sin and death that distort creation once good at its beginning. The future rule of God breaks in ahead of time as a harbinger of the world's future to be fully and finally reconciled to God."[23] But although inaugurated by Jesus, God's kingdom will come in fullness only when he returns, a final victory that the Gospels describe using apocalyptic language. Meanwhile, the kingdom of God is on its way and there is a gospel to proclaim.

---

21. Wright, *Simply Good News*, 55. Italics original.
22. McKnight, *Kingdom Conspiracy*, 135.
23. Hunsberger, "Missional Vocation," 91.

GOD'S KINGDOM, MISSION, AND CONGREGATIONS

For the exegetes and the GOCN theologians whom I have quoted, Jesus is central to God's kingdom, and God's kingdom or rule is central to the Bible, introduced in Genesis, with its final restoration anticipated in the book of Revelation. But how does the kingdom of God relate to respect for congregations, which is the key concern of this book? The GOCN theologians root their respect for congregations in their conviction that congregations play a vital role in the time between Jesus's inauguration of God's kingdom and its final arrival when he returns in glory. That brings us back to a question introduced earlier, What are congregations for?

Recall from chapter 3 that Anthony Robinson identified the traditional purpose of mainline American Protestant congregations as being a community's conscience, its instrument of aid, and a center for its community and family life. Such purposes are commendable, but as Robinson noted, they are not intrinsically Christian; besides, those purposes are increasingly fulfilled by a range of alternative agencies. Where I live, a community center offers people of all ages exercise classes, various support groups, library services, and a café where friends and neighbors can gather. Such centers across the continent leave thousands of declining congregations with their traditional roles—some of them more distinctly Christian than Robinson allows—feeling that they have lost their way and asking, "What are we here for? What is our purpose?" Anthony Robinson proposes a better purpose for American congregations: "To bring about change in people's lives" by means of personal conversion and discipleship.[24] Though more reflective of the New Testament, this purpose is still too small, for as the GOCN theologians insist, respect for congregations lies in the conviction that they have a role to play in the final reestablishment of God's kingdom. It is challenging, however, for congregations to see themselves in relation to the vast scale involved in the reestablishing of God's rule. Facing that challenge, some theological liberals reduce the kingdom to good people working to rid the world of a range of social ills, even if their work is unrelated to Jesus's redemptive work or the church, and it leads some theological conservatives to reduce the kingdom to Jesus "ruling in my heart," or locating it far off in the future. But for Jesus, God's kingdom is what life is about and what God's people are about: "Strive first for the kingdom of God," he said (Matt 6:33); pray above all else, "Your kingdom come . . . on earth as it is in heaven"

---

24. Robinson, *Transforming Congregational Culture*, 32.

Theological Respect for Congregations

(Matt 6:10). With the book of Revelation in mind, N. T. Wright conveys the scale of God's kingdom in these words:

> The biblical writers live with the tension of believing both that in one sense God has always been sovereign over the world and that in another sense this sovereignty, this saving rule, is something which must break afresh into the world of corruption, decay, and death, and the human rebellion, idolatry, and sin which are so closely linked to it . . . . When Revelation speaks of God and the Lamb receiving all power, glory, honor, and so forth, it is because through the Lamb's victory the whole creation is being brought back into its intended harmony, rescued from evil and death.[25]

Now, a vast distance may seem to separate God's kingdom as outlined above from local North American congregations worried by dull sermons, rising insurance rates, and the absence of kids. But the distance is less daunting if we recall how the book of Revelation links seven struggling first-century congregations in Asia Minor to a time when "the kingdom of the world has become the kingdom of our Lord and of his Messiah" (Rev 11:15). Even flawed congregations are linked to the kingdom of God; in fact, their true purpose is to witness to the coming kingdom of God. Andrew Root and Blair Bertrand, authors of *When Church Stops Working*, quoted in chapter 2, helpfully write that "just because the church is not the star does not mean it has no role to play. Best Supporting Actor is an important Oscar category. The church is essential, but only as it realizes and confesses that it is not the star of its own story . . . . The story the church is living is not primarily about the church at all! The church lives for a bigger story."[26] That story, say the GOCN theologians, is the kingdom of God. If so, far from being free agents who can be or do whatever they wish, congregations "belong to Christ" (1 Cor 3:23) and are called to be local agents of Christ's kingdom.

But just how do congregations relate to the kingdom of God? Most helpful in providing an answer to that question is the missionary statesman Lesslie Newbigin. Influenced by Karl Barth's theological respect for the church and for congregations, he handed on that respect to the GOCN theologians. To Newbigin's thinking about the church and congregations I now turn.

---

25. Wright, *Scripture and the Authority*, 27.
26. Root and Bertrand, *When Church Stops Working*, 75.

Respecting Congregations

In his 1953 book, *The Household of God*, Newbigin affirms the Reformation claim that faith in Christ is what reconciles us to God, a faith evoked by the power of Word and Sacraments. He appreciatively quotes Calvin: "Whenever we see the word of God sincerely preached and heard, whenever we see the sacraments administered according to the institution of Christ, there we cannot have any doubt that the Church of God has some existence."[27] Though not intended, the Reformation emphasis on the church as a place for preaching and sacraments led over time, says Newbigin, to congregations being regarded as places where things happen. George Hunsberger adds, "This perception of the church gives little attention to the church as a communal entity or presence [and] stresses even less the community's role as the bearer of missional responsibility."[28] Accordingly, North America's voluntarist congregations, competing for members in the late twentieth century, marketed themselves to attract new or retain old members to attend "places where things happen."

Newbigin and Hunsberger both say that Protestants have lost touch with New Testament ways of understanding congregations. Though some congregations may take seriously the ministry of Word and Sacraments, writes Newbigin, they do not take seriously the apostle Paul's teaching that the church as the body of Christ is to represent Christ to the world in local congregations "where the light of God really shines and the life of God really pulses."[29] After all, says Newbigin, what Jesus left behind, rather than a book, creed, system of thought, or rule of life, was a community, a visible "company of men and women with ascertainable names and addresses.... It was present on the day of Pentecost, and the Lord added to it day by day those that are being saved."[30] Reflecting on 1 Corinthians, Newbigin insists that though far from being "some ideal and invisible entity," Corinth's congregation was "an actual congregation... whose life was marked by all the grievous sins of which the apostle has to speak."[31] And yet Paul called it the body of Christ.

Newbigin deeply respects the role of congregations in God's mission to reestablish the kingdom of God. In *Sign of the Kingdom*, he notes, for example, how the word *arrabon*, used three times in Paul's letters and

---

27. Newbigin, *Household of God*, 49.
28. Hunsberger, "Missional Vocation," 80.
29. Newbigin, *Household of God*, 56.
30. Newbigin, *Household of God*, 27.
31. Newbigin, *Household of God*, 71.

Theological Respect for Congregations

translated in the NRSV by three different words—"pledge," "guarantee," and "installment"—links the church to God's mission and kingdom. *Arrabon*, used in Greek life to mean installment, is a clue, says Newbigin, to how Paul understood Pentecost as the moment when the church received the Spirit as a pledge, guarantee, or first installment of more to come—that "more" being God's coming kingdom. For Paul, writes Newbigin, the *arrabon* is God's gift of the Spirit that empowers the church to witness to Jesus, a witness that isn't "an accomplishment of the Church" but the work of the Spirit.[32] As to the kingdom of God, Newbigin suggests that it is neither separated from nor identified with the church; rather, the "presence of God in the company of believers is given as the veritable foretaste and first fruit of the kingdom and . . . as the witness of the reality of the Kingdom."[33]

In his book *The Gospel in a Pluralist Society*, Newbigin further elucidates the role of congregations in relation to God's kingdom and mission in a chapter titled "The Congregation as Hermeneutic of the Gospel." Knowing the fragility of post-Christendom congregations in the UK and in North America, Newbigin nevertheless places his hope in congregations. He writes:

> The primary reality of which we have to take account in seeking for a Christian impact on public life is the Christian congregation. How is it possible that the gospel should be credible, that people should come to believe that the power which has the last word in human affairs is represented by a man hanging on a cross? I am suggesting that the only answer, the only hermeneutic of the gospel, is a congregation of men and women who believe it and live by it. I am, of course, not denying the importance of the many activities by which we seek to challenge public life with the gospel—evangelistic campaigns, distribution of Bibles and Christian literature, conferences, and even books such as this one. But I am saying that these are all secondary, and that they have power to accomplish their purpose only as they are rooted in and lead back to a believing community.[34]

Newbigin then movingly describes a congregation as a community that praises God for his grace, a community committed to "the constant remembering and rehearsing of the true story of human nature and destiny," a community "that does not live for itself but is deeply involved in . . . its neighborhood," a community "from which good news overflows into good

---

32. Newbigin, *Sign of the Kingdom*, 38.
33. Newbigin, *Sign of the Kingdom*, 41.
34. Newbigin, *Gospel in a Pluralist Society*, 227.

action," a community "where men and women are prepared . . . to stand before people on behalf of God," a community of hope that is "the foretaste of a different social order . . . in which the reality of the new creation is present, known, and experienced, and from which men and women will go into every sector of public life to claim it for Christ." Such a congregation, says Newbigin, is "the sign, instrument, and foretaste of God's redeeming grace for the whole life of society."[35]

Newbigin presents a compelling purpose for congregations that relates them directly to the kingdom of God and to its king. The good news of the kingdom is not just that God desires to see life on earth transformed, the view of idealistic social gospelers a century ago, but that Jesus placed himself at the center of the kingdom he proclaimed. This is clear in Luke 4:16–19, which reports how Jesus once read and reacted to the prophetic words of Isaiah in a synagogue:

> "The Spirit of the Lord is upon me, because he has anointed me to bring good news to the poor. He has sent me to proclaim release to the captives and recovery of sight to the blind, to let the oppressed go free, to proclaim the year of the Lord's favor." And he rolled up the scroll, gave it back to the attendant, and sat down. The eyes of all in the synagogue were fixed on him. Then he began to say to them, "Today this scripture has been fulfilled in your hearing."

For Newbigin and the GOCN theologians, the kingdom of God is not a free-floating social project; the kingdom is about the sovereign God coming to reign and doing so through Jesus. Christopher Wright puts it like this: "The kingdom of God is at work in and through the lives of those who have 'entered' it, that is, in whose lives God is reigning through repentance and faith in Christ, in those who are committed to the ways of Jesus Christ by submitting to him as Lord, in those who seek first the kingdom of God and his justice, in those who hunger and thirst for justice."[36] Love, forgiveness, peace-making, holiness, justice—all central to God's kingdom—are defined in relation to the life, death, resurrection, and final return of Jesus. As to congregations, their purpose is to represent in their neighborhoods, even if imperfectly, God's rule inaugurated by Jesus. As usual, Newbigin cuts through a good deal of fuzzy thinking with these words: "The question which has to be put to every local congregation is the question whether it is a credible sign of God's reign in justice and mercy over the whole of

---

35. Newbigin, *Gospel in a Pluralist Society*, 229–33.
36. Wright, *Mission of God's People*, 187.

life, whether it is an open fellowship whose concerns are as wide as the concerns of humanity, whether it cares for its neighbours in a way which reflects and springs out of God's care for them, whether its common life is recognizable as a foretaste of the blessing which God intends for the whole human family."[37]

Inspired by Newbigin, the contributors to *Missional Church* agree that North American congregations must understand that the mission to which they are called is not their own project supported by their own financial resources. No, congregations are called to partner in God's mission narrated in God's word. Beginning with God's promise to Abraham and Sarah that God will bless the nations through them (Gen 12), God's mission continues with God calling Israel to be God's light to the nations (Isa 49:6), reaches a turning point when God sent Jesus to inaugurate God's rule over the nations through his death and resurrection, and expands when God sends the Holy Spirit to empower believing congregations to witness to the nations that Jesus is their Lord and Savior (Acts 1:8). Rather than conceiving of mission as the church extending itself or saving individual souls out of the world, God's mission, say the GOCN theologians, is about how God's Son will reestablish God's kingdom.

Congregations, then, are not called to be vendors of religious goods and services, but to be a people sent to the world to witness to Christ and his kingdom. Far from being a mere church department, mission is the very essence of the church; it is what congregations are for! Neither, in this theocentric understanding of mission, say the GOCN theologians, is mission a church-inspired project. To the contrary, mission springs from God's being, particularly God's trinitarian being. Darrell Guder approvingly quotes the South African missiologist David Bosch: "Mission [is] . . . derived from the very nature of God . . . God the Father sending the Son, and God the Father and the Son sending the Spirit . . . [and] yet another 'movement': Father, Son and Holy Spirit sending the church into the world."[38] Sometimes taken for granted by conservatives and bypassed by liberals, the Trinity has been a major item for discussion in recent ecumenical dialogue involving Eastern Orthodoxy; the outcome has been the embrace by Protestant theologians of the ancient, patristic insight that at the core of God's being is a communion of love that forever flows between the three persons of the Trinity.[39]

---

37. Newbigin, *Sign of the Kingdom*, 64.
38. Guder, "Missional Church," 5.
39. For a brief overview of recent trinitarian thinking, see Richardson, "Contemporary

But how does this seemingly esoteric insight help congregations? Recent study of God's trinitarian nature highlights that, though one, God is not solitary but is a community of Father, Son, and Spirit. In their book, *Participating in God's Mission*, Craig Van Gelder and Dwight Zscheile see the eternal communion that flows within the inner life of the Trinity and flowing out to a humanity turned against God "as a response to this predicament of broken communion."[40] The turning point in the unfolding to the world of God's trinitarian and missional character, say Van Gelder and Zscheile, was the incarnation of the Son of God. It "speaks of God's life and truth becoming enfleshed in the specific, unique, and local," and offers congregations a pattern for the unfolding of their neighborhood mission: "It is in the local and concrete, not the abstract, where we join up with what God is doing to restore community in Christ in the power of the Spirit."[41]

It is this level of theological respect for congregations that can help them to engage and witness to their local neighborhoods, rather than being places that offer people exhausting religious programs, activities, and services. Instead of competing with others in a market-driven, consumerist society, congregations should seize the opportunity, say Van Gelder and Zscheile, "to reclaim the incarnation and re-enter the spaces of neighborhood life in simpler ways. The church does not need to compete with the entertainment and shopping industries on their terms. Ordinary disciples can indwell local relationships and spaces as Jesus did."[42]

God's trinitarian life, then, is not at all esoteric, but is the source of the divine love that the Holy Spirit pours out to empower the mission of local congregations. I suspect, however, that what motivated the efforts to fix congregations in the decades following the 1960s cultural revolution, at least in part, was a desire to reclaim the worldly power and success that North American churches had long enjoyed. When so tempted, congregational leaders must resist worldly success, as Jesus did (Matt 4:1–11), and recognize and respect the shape of Jesus's ministry outlined in a text like Phil 2:5–11, namely, that the eternal Son, who eternally enjoyed the flow of love within the Trinity, "did not regard equality with God as something to be exploited, but emptied himself . . . humbled himself and became obedient to the point of death." I hope I am saying what Scot McKnight meant

---

Renewal," 183–92.

40. Van Gelder and Zscheile, *Participating in God's Mission*, 268–69.
41. Van Gelder and Zscheile, *Participating in God's Mission*, 272.
42. Van Gelder and Zscheile, *Participating in God's Mission*, 273.

by the word "Christoformity"—that God calls and gives congregations the power to serve as Christ served.

Contemplating how the communion of love that flows between the Father, Son, and Spirit empowers the local mission of congregations, makes me joyful and hopeful. Imagine it: Ordinary congregations with ordinary, everyday ministries related to and fueled by the supernatural life of the triune God. Sometimes a congregation feels like a lonely "monad," distant both from other congregations and from its own neighborhood. The doctrine of the Trinity, however, though it may seem distant from local congregations, offers them a source of joy as they realize that the eternal love that flows within God's trinitarian being flows to them to empower their participation in God's mission. If God is real, and if God's nature is trinitarian, then a congregation is far more than meets the eye! No wonder the apostle Paul, who called Corinth's congregation the body of Christ, had such respect for congregations!

With respect for congregations still in mind, I return to Hunsberger's essay in *Missional Church*, which proposes that the purpose of congregations is to represent the kingdom of God as its *community, servant,* and *messenger.* Knowing how Jesus embodied the reign of God by living under its authority and resisting temptations to do otherwise, the church as the kingdom's *community* must likewise embody the reign of God by living under its authority, displaying "the first-fruits of the forgiven and forgiving people of God who are brought across the rubble of dividing walls that have crumbled under the weight of the cross."[43] That sentence suggests that a congregation's witness is effective only if its corporate life is credible in the eyes of the watching world; as Hunsberger says, "God has designed it so that when people have seen God's 'peculiar' people, they have in a real sense caught a view of God."[44]

As to being the kingdom's *servant*, the church must act like Jesus, writes Hunsberger; like a servant, Jesus was "predisposed to be interrupted . . . whenever hunger, sickness, demonic oppression, the grip of sin, social ostracism, or death crossed his path." So, acts of compassion from individual Christians will join the vital and larger ministries of peace-making, compassion, and justice through which, says Hunsberger, congregations can "bring wholeness and dignity to the world and thereby provide a taste of the future in the reign of God under the rule and authority of

---

43. Hunsberger, "Missional Vocation," 103.
44. Hunsberger, "Missional Vocation," 104.

Christ's lordship."[45] Though the kingdom of God is not primarily a social or political program, Christian congregations are to live out its social and political implications by praying for and serving God's rule on earth, as it is in heaven.

As to being the kingdom's *messenger*, the church must, like Jesus, says Hunsberger, use words to convey the meaning of Jesus's person and ministry; otherwise, the church remains anonymous and ambiguous. However, "Verbalizing the gospel of Jesus removes the ambiguity. It also renders the reign of God accessible." After all, "if in our being the church, the world *sees* God's reign, and by our doing justice, the world *tastes* its gracious effect, then the call to all on the earth to receive and acknowledge that reign begs to be expressed."[46]

Understanding the church as called to *embody*, *exhibit*, and *express* the good news of God's kingdom, congregations witness locally to the ultimate reality for which we pray, the coming of the kingdom of God. Hunsberger puts it like this: "Churches are called to be bodies of people sent on a mission rather than the storefronts for vendors of religious services and goods . . . . We must surrender the self-conception of the church as a voluntary association of individuals and live by the recognition that we are a communal body of Christ's followers, mutually committed and responsible to one another and to the mission Jesus set us upon at his resurrection."[47]

Hunsberger and the GOCN theologians are agreed that the corporate purpose of the church is to witness to the kingdom of God, a purpose obscured during the Christendom era. But for the church and for congregations to offer Christian witness to the world, they need to differ from the world, a point Jesus made when, in the Sermon on the Mount, he spoke of choosing the hard rather than the easy road, of being wise rather than foolish builders, and of learning to pray differently, not heaping "up empty phrases as the Gentiles do" (Matt 6:7). Likewise, the apostle Paul, eager for congregations to take seriously their missional purpose, insists that they be different: "Do not be conformed to this world but be transformed by the renewing of your minds" (Rom 12:2), or "this I affirm and insist on in the Lord: you must no longer live as the Gentiles live" (Eph 4:17), or "Do not be mismatched with unbelievers. For what partnership is there between righteousness and lawlessness? Or what fellowship is there between light

---

45. Hunsberger, "Missional Vocation," 106.
46. Hunsberger, "Missional Vocation," 107–8.
47. Hunsberger, "Missional Vocation," 108.

and darkness?" (2 Cor 6:14). In other places, Paul writes more positively of the world than those verses suggest; nevertheless, he saw congregations as distinctively different, God-delivered communities. In Col 1:13 he tells a congregation that God "has rescued us from the power of darkness and transferred us into the kingdom of his beloved Son, in whom we have redemption, the forgiveness of sins."

Congregations that respect the identity and purpose of congregations as presented in the New Testament and clarified by the GOCN theologians embrace a vocation as outposts of the kingdom of God. As such, they are called to partake in God's life, know God's pardon, discover God's power to break down the walls that divide human society, and experience God's Spirit helping them to embody, exhibit, and express the good news of the kingdom of which Jesus is king. It is true that individual Christians are called to a holy life that witnesses to Jesus, yet the focus of the New Testament is on corporate, congregational witness. Darrell Guder writes, "It is essential for the called community to understand that its common conduct before a 'watching world' [John Howard Yoder!] is its first and most powerful form of witness to the gospel."[48] This understanding, however, will feel foreign to most of North America's Christendom-era congregations.

I have underlined that congregations are local outposts of the kingdom inaugurated by Jesus's death and resurrection, but at the same time, the kingdom Jesus inaugurated remains incomplete. If a congregation emphasizes God's kingdom and the Spirit's gifts as already present but ignores the "not yet" of the kingdom, the congregation's sense of triumph may blind it to its capacity for sin. On the other hand, if a congregation emphasizes that God's kingdom is not yet present in fullness and downplays the Spirit's gifts already given, its tentativeness about God's present power may weaken its witness. I recall in the 1990s that a few members of the Toronto congregation that I served, sensing that our congregation was spiritually tepid, attended the charismatic Toronto Airport Vineyard Church to experience more of the "already." At the same time, some folk from that Vineyard Church showed up in our congregation, seeking a place where their sorrow and loss, reflecting the "not yet" of God's kingdom, were allowed to be expressed. Congregations, it seems, need to respect the fact that there is some distance between what they are now and the future to which they aspire and point.

---

48. Guder, *Called to Witness*, 109.

SOME QUESTIONS FOR THE MISSIONAL THEOLOGIANS

The kingdom-oriented, missional thinking of the GOCN theologians is for me a marvelous source of respect for congregations, but I want to raise a few concerns. First, what Hunsberger and other missional theologians have called for during the first quarter of the twenty-first century—that congregations respect their purpose as missional communities—has not penetrated most North America's congregations; too many of them, isolated within their neighborhoods, continue to function as religious clubs where old friends meet. Though they may corporately enjoy Sunday worship or corporately raise funds for a special ministry, few mainline Protestant congregations see themselves as called to corporately embody, exhibit, and express the good news of God's kingdom to their neighbors. The longstanding privatization and individualization of faith in North American congregations inhibits such a missional purpose.

Another concern is that since the publishing of *Missional Church*, the word "missional" has lost much of its early meaning. I once heard one member of a congregation claim that having upgraded its parking, his congregation was now missional. Alan Roxburgh, a *Missional Church* contributor, complains that missional has become "an adjectival modifier for practically everything congregations and denominations do" and that "the movement has widely been turned into a series of tactics for church renewal, growth, and health, despite its founders' best intentions."[49] Turning Christendom congregations into missional congregations isn't for the faint of heart. Far from offering a quick fix, the GOCN theologians demand that congregations consider the biblical narrative of God's mission that focuses on the coming of God's kingdom, and then rethink, reframe, and respect their identity and purpose. Darrell Guder comments that what missional theologians offer the church is "a massive critique of the Christendom theology project."[50] How true!

But I have yet another concern: in discussing the work of the GOCN theologians, I often used the word "congregation" where they did not. Though this word is an important one for Newbigin, it is rare in GOCN material. I understand this to a point, for missional theology is to an extent produced by seminary-based theologians, not congregational leaders; their task has been to theologically enrich the church rather than write how-to

---

49. Roxburgh, *Joining God, Remaking Church*, 21.
50. Guder, *Called to Witness*, 24.

books for congregations. Yet I wonder if the decision made by contributors to the Guder-edited *Missional Church*—to use the terms "church" and "missional community" and drop the word "congregation"—may help to explain why their insights as to how the church connects to God's kingdom, mission, and trinitarian nature have not penetrated North American congregations. The GOCN theologians no doubt hoped that in launching the word "missional" a generation ago, and renaming congregations as "missional communities," they would encourage a fresh sense of purpose within local churches. I have a high regard for Guder and his fellow missional theologians, but their decision to abandon the word "congregation" was likely to puzzle the millions of people who populate North America's congregations, no matter how accurate the term "missional community" is. Nor are clergy likely to welcome folk to Sunday worship with the words, "Welcome to our congreg—oops, missional community." After all, the word "congregation" carries deep meaning that goes back to the Old Testament's congregation of Israel; to persecuted New Testament congregations; and to the millions of local, flawed, but well-loved congregations that have populated the globe ever since.

Guder explains in *Missional Church* that its contributors set the word "congregation" aside because it suggests an outdated geographical parish system; conveys a Christendom-era maintenance mentality; and evokes a church nominalism that makes membership thresholds meaningless.[51] There is truth in this characterization, compared with which the idea of a missional community must have sounded fresh and intentional in 1998. But ironically, "community" now feels as dated as "congregation," and the word "church," which the GOCN collaborators agreed to retain, has almost as many negative associations as the word "congregation."

More damaging to the GOCN missional project is that the decision to call a congregation a "missional community" makes it hard for leaders and members in North American congregations, already rather distant from theologians, to recognize themselves in the writing of the GOCN theologians. That said, in his 2015 book, *Called to Witness*, Darrell Guder, though he still prefers "missional community," allows the word "congregation" to return, as does Alan Roxburgh in his 2015 book, *Joining God, Remaking Church, Changing the World*.

Admittedly, the term "missional community" rightly promotes the GOCN insight that congregations, though ready to gather, must also scatter

---

51. See Guder, "Missional Structures," 234–44.

to serve God's mission. As to their sending vocation, "missional community" is preferable to the word "congregation," which refers to a gathering. But the opposite is also true: the term "missional community" does not evoke what the Bible says about the need for congregations to gather. If it is a fact that many gathered congregations ignore the idea of being sent, the opposite danger is that Christians who scatter to do "kingdom" work in the world sometimes avoid gathering in congregations. Van Gelder and Zscheile warn that this very thing—Christians working for the good of the world, who do not gather for worship and fellowship—may lead to "the secularization of the kingdom" and the "loss of ecclesial identity."[52]

Dare I suggest that within Godself, the Father, Son, and Holy Spirit "congregate" and then "scatter" in mission to the world? At any rate, to balance the need for congregations to gather for formation and then scatter for mission, I propose the term "missional congregation" as respectfully recognizable. Perhaps Darrell Guder might agree, for in *Called to Witness* he writes, "The inescapable conclusion of the missional reading of the Bible is that God is carrying out his saving and healing purposes for the world through gathered communities, through congregations," and adds that "the primary task of a missional hermeneutic . . . is to provide a particular congregation the formation it needs to be able to live out both its gathered life and its scattered life faithfully."[53] I respond with the nontheological word "Bingo!"

Having vented my concerns, I note that congregations across Canada and the USA continue to unravel. Proposals keep appearing as to how to stop the unraveling, one being that it is time for congregations to jettison long-established congregational and adjudicatory structures in favor of small, organic groups, on the assumption that institutional structures inhibit creativity. It is too early to say where this, or the current interest in post-denominational congregations, may lead, but Van Gelder and Zscheile warn that the notion that church structures can be set aside may be historically naive and reflect "the expressive individualism of late modernity."[54]

I wrote in the introduction that I have no easy answers for North America's declining congregations, yet I am not prepared to give up on them. At the same time, given that North Americans tend to be wired for action, suspicious of history, and addicted to change, I view with caution calls for congregations to forget the old and to enter a new world where

---

52. Van Gelder and Zscheile, *Participating in God's Mission*, 276.
53. Guder, *Called to Witness*, 109 and 116.
54. Van Gelder and Zscheile, *Participating in God's Mission*, 303.

none have gone before. On the one hand, weary congregations should trust God to help them navigate an unknown future and not fear ecclesial experiments that respect the theological identity and missional purpose that I have sketched for them, based on the GOCN theologians; on the other hand, congregations that relish risk-taking and the pursuit of all that is new should recall Alister McGrath's reminder that tradition helps the church to be faithful to the gospel.

CONCLUSION

The Newbigin-inspired GOCN theologians urge congregations to find their identity and purpose in relation to God's kingdom and God's mission, as communities of God that share in the transformative life of the triune God through the Holy Spirit, who in turn empowers them to live and to witness to Jesus as local colonies of God's kingdom. This respects congregations in a more fundamental way than do functionalist understandings of congregations and offers them, in whatever culture or context they are placed, a Bible-narrated missional purpose. Of course, it is true that God uses non-congregational agencies in mission, whether the Bible, personal witness, Christian literature, parachurch agencies, and even theological argument; nevertheless, it is praising, forgiving, learning, witnessing, hospitable, imperfect congregations that God calls to carry God's mission forward and pass on the Christian faith. God's way of salvation, says Newbigin, means that "the broken harmony between all men and between man and God and man and nature, must be communicated . . . by the actual development of a community which embodies—if only in foretaste—the restored harmony of which it speaks. A gospel of reconciliation can only be communicated by a reconciled fellowship."[55]

So, rather than despair about the future of congregations, I encourage their leaders to read the work of Newbigin, Guder, Van Gelder, Hunsberger, Roxburgh, and others, even as I hope that a new generation of missional theologians will update and add to the work of the GOCN, making their material as accessible as possible to congregations. Meanwhile, chapter 5 will explore how congregations can respect both their gathered and scattered local ministries, a ministry pattern already hinted at in this chapter.

I close with this much-told and much-emended story about Pope John XXIII, the twentieth century's most innovative pope. As such, he bore

---

55. Newbigin, *Household of God*, 141.

heavy responsibilities, yet he was a man of deep humility. We're told that in his nightly prayers, during which he unburdened himself to God, he heard God say, "But who governs the church, Angelo? Is it you or me?" He admitted that it was not him and then heard God say, "Very well then. Sleep well, Angelo. Sleep well."

5

Respecting Congregational Ministry

FRUSTRATING TO SOME BUT fascinating to most, congregations come in a wide variety. No two are the same: some are old, some are new, some are formal, and others not. They may be small, medium, or large; urban, suburban, or rural; denominational or nondenominational; progressive or fundamentalist—and so on. Behind this variety lies the fact that congregations are, to some extent, free to make choices, often secondary in nature rather than primary. The first assignment of the worship course I used to teach was to have students visit a local congregation and analyze that congregation's worship. I recall that one student noted that Jesus was named only once in the worship service of the congregation he visited. My response was this: "That congregation has made a conscious choice, for you have to work hard to ensure that Jesus's name is rarely used in the worship of a Christian congregation."

Considering the many choices that congregations are free to make, my book has proposed that there are some givens that congregations ought to accept and respect if they are to be truly Christian. Recall that to respect something is, in the words of Robin Dillon, "to heed its call, accord it its due, acknowledge its claim."[1] In previous chapters, I articulated two congregational givens to be respected: that a congregation is a local "in Christ" community that confesses Jesus as Lord, and that a congregation is a local

---

1. Dillon, "Respect," §1.1.

community that witnesses to Jesus as it serves God's kingdom and mission. If free in many ways to shape its life, a congregation is not free to dilute its christological identity or missional purpose.

Given that identity and purpose, and aware of how varied congregations are, the New Testament goes on to articulate a third given that ought to be respected: a pattern for congregational ministry. This ministry pattern, which in practical ways expresses the identity and purpose of New Testament congregations, has two basic movements: gathering to be formed as God's people, and scattering as God's people to serve God's mission. As Darrell Guder says, the work of the apostles was "to provide a particular congregation the formation it needs to be able to live out both its gathered life and its scattered life faithfully."[2]

This gathering/scattering pattern appears in the Gospels; for example, Matt 10:1–15 and Luke 10:1–12 tell how Jesus gathered his disciples and then scattered them to witness to God's kingdom. In line with this, Matt 28:7–8 reports that the angel who told the women who visited Jesus's tomb that he had risen spoke four gathering/scattering words: Come! See! Go! Tell! The same pattern appears in John 20:21, in which Jesus tells his gathered disciples, "As the Father has sent me, so I send you," and reappears in Acts 1:8, when Jesus tells the same gathered disciples to wait until they receive the Spirit to empower their witness to him "in Jerusalem, in all Judea and Samaria and to the ends of the earth." Acts 2 then describes how Jerusalem's post-Pentecost congregation gathered to devote itself "to the apostles' teaching and fellowship, to the breaking of bread and the prayers" (Acts 2:42) and then scattered into local neighborhoods, in the process gaining "the good will of all the people" and growing as "day by day the Lord added to their number those who were being saved" (Acts 2:47). Though Acts 8:1–4 later reports that persecution led some of those believers to scatter "throughout . . . Judea and Samaria," back then and now, most believers scatter more locally.

Paul's letters also assume that congregations will gather to be formed in Christ and scatter as his witnesses; thus, he writes at Col 4:16 that he expects Colossae's believers to gather to hear his letter to them. That letter does three important things; it reiterates the congregation's identity—"no longer Greek and Jew, circumcised and uncircumcised, barbarian, Scythian, slave and free . . . God's chosen ones, holy and beloved" (Col 3:11–12)—promotes the congregation's ongoing formation through gathered ministry—"clothe

---

2. Guder, *Called to Witness*, 116.

yourselves with compassion, kindness, humility, meekness, and patience. Bear with one another.... Let the word of Christ dwell in you richly; teach and admonish one another ... sing psalms, hymns, and spiritual songs to God" (Col 3:12–16)—and then advises how the congregation ought to go about its scattered ministry among unbelievers—"Conduct yourselves wisely toward outsiders, making the most of the time. Let your speech always be gracious, seasoned with salt, so that you may know how to answer everyone" (Col 4:5–6).

The gathering/scattering ministry pattern of the New Testament, which this chapter will explore, is formally endorsed by the following words taken from the Presbyterian Church in Canada's liturgy when ordaining its clergy and elders:

> All ministries of the Church proceed from and are sustained by the ministry of the Lord Jesus Christ. He is our Prophet, Priest and king, the Minister of the covenant of grace. By the operation of God's Word and Spirit, the Church is gathered, equipped, and sent out to participate in this ministry. All members of the Church are to share the Gospel with the world, and to offer to the Father the worship and service that are due to the Creator from the creation, through Christ, the only Mediator, until he comes again.[3]

But, when it comes to the New Testament's gathered/scattered ministry pattern, North American congregations do not always "heed its call" or "accord it its due." Unaware of the identity, purpose, and ministry pattern the New Testament offers them, some congregations stumble and find it difficult to minister with confidence, or at all.

But there is more at stake than whether congregations are confident: Congregations belong and are accountable to God, something that is not always how North American congregations think of themselves. It is true that God uses humans to build congregations, yet the New Testament thinks of them as owned and led by God—Paul calls Corinth's believers "the church of God" (1 Cor 1:2), Jesus famously said, "I will build my church" (Matt 16:18), and Col 1:18 names Christ as "the head of the body, the church," a headship that is real when congregations respect their christological identity, missional purpose, and gathering/scattering ministry pattern.

As to this gathering/scattering ministry pattern, in my experience, most congregations like to gather but are less keen to scatter. Indeed, Christendom-era congregations assumed that their scattering was unnecessary since North

---

3. Presbyterian Church in Canada, *Book of Common Worship*, 392.

America was already Christian. In addition, the Reformation conviction—that Protestant congregations needed to have their "Catholic" understanding of the gospel corrected by Bible-based preaching—created gathered congregations being taught the apostolic scriptures while they ignored the scattered ministry of the actual apostles, The result made church a place where things happen, not a body that scatters in mission to the community.

RESPECTING THE GATHERED MINISTRY OF CONGREGATIONS

To respect the gathering/scattering pattern of congregational ministry that the New Testament offers involves discussing more practical aspects of congregational life than in previous chapters. I begin with gathering ministries. A good deal of congregational ministry could be considered as gathered: youth ministry, fellowship groups, Bible studies, pastoral care, and even pickleball! But rather than tackle all of that, I focus on what most congregations gather for: the ministry of preaching and worship.

Donald Coggin, Anglican archbishop of York (1961–74), was once invited to preach at the dedication of a refurbished Anglican church whose grand feature "was the altar, central and resplendent."[4] When Coggin asked where he was to preach from, he was told that a "little stand" would appear at that point in the service. Coggin later informed the architect that worship furniture should reflect the two primary means of grace in the Church of England, the sacrament of the Word and Table. I might have gone further to argue that, theologically, the pulpit precedes the table.

But while worship furniture guarantees little—high pulpit preachers don't always compel and some who preach at a "little stand" do—worship furniture nevertheless matters. A pulpit tells how God spoke "to our ancestors in many and various ways by the prophets [and] by a Son" (Heb 1:1–2) and still speaks through preachers. A baptismal font tells how in baptism Jesus began his ministry by identifying with the sinners for whom he would later die and recalls that Jesus told his disciples to make disciples, "baptizing them in the name of the Father, Son, and Holy Spirit" (Matt 28:19). A communion table tells how Jesus both used bread and wine to signify his death and commanded that we use bread and wine to feed on him until the kingdom of God is consummated with a heavenly feast. If worship

---

4. Coggin, *Sacrament of the Word*, 24.

furniture tells how God made and still makes himself known in Jesus, its place in worship deserves to be respected.

Let's first think about how to respect the ministry of preaching and its power to form and transform gathered congregations. Traditional Protestants prioritize the pulpit, believing that through preaching, God's word releases God's power to convert, counsel, and correct God's people. I suspect, however, that North American Protestant congregations are no longer sure their pulpits have that power. In some churches, pulpits, tables, and fonts are removed, leaving a stage dominated by a praise band; in others, a decline in respect for preaching is signaled by the fact that the pews have emptied out, leading David Read to comment that discouraged preachers might want to reverse the apostle Paul's line, "how shall they hear without a preacher?" with "how shall they preach without a hearer?"[5] But rather than debate why preaching has lost respect, I will suggest that to increase respect for preaching that builds up God's people, preachers must respect words, listeners, the Bible, and both God's and their own roles in the ministry of preaching.

Think about the words preachers use. As attendance at worship declined during the 1960s, some traced that decline to wordy, religious language: "When [people] are accustomed to the swiftly moving images of the screen, how can we expect them to give their attention to one person talking, with no frills, no light relief, and nothing else to look at?" writes John Stott.[6] Yet the transformative power of words remains, evident in those of twentieth-century leaders such as Churchill, Solzhenitsyn, Martin Luther King, and Mandela. As Stott says, "though doves can coo, donkeys bray, monkeys squeal, and pigs grunt, only human beings can speak."[7] So, rather than being intimidated by words, preachers should respect their capacity to form congregations.

David Buttrick's 1987 book, *Homiletic: Moves and Structures*, examines the words that preachers use in great detail. Buttrick reminds us that "faith comes from what is heard" (Rom 10:17) and adds that words give us our humanity, tell us stories, give us our identity, and can rename the world as God's world.[8] But preachers, says Buttrick, do not always respect the power of words to deliver the gospel and continue to use pious, theological language without asking whether it carries the meaning it once did. I notice

---

5. Read, *Sent from God*, 15.
6. Stott, *I Believe in Preaching*, 75.
7. Stott, *I Believe in Preaching*, 75.
8. Buttrick, *Homiletic*, 7.

this when I return to Ireland and hear sermons that, eager to be faithful to the Bible, use traditional preaching language that sometimes sounds stale. Aware of this happening in North America, Buttrick calls preachers to exchange their traditional vocabulary for the more colloquial, metaphorical language that Jesus used in his parables to help listeners to "see" as well as hear the gospel.

Buttrick's critics warn, however, that proposals to replace theological language with more metaphorical language may lead to a loss of theological precision. I noted earlier Andrew Purves's fear that the term "self-actualization" is not the same as salvation, and I now note Tom Long's fear that the word "acceptance" does not do justice to what the Bible means by grace.[9] The American preacher William Willimon, though no fan of clichés, calls the church to claim its own story and speech, ethos, and practices: "To preach among the baptized . . . is to operate within a domain of distinctive discourse. We talk differently here."[10]

Respect for words is complex, for sermons ought, said St. Augustine, "to teach, to delight, and to persuade."[11] In addition, a preacher's words must resonate with twenty-first-century listeners but also faithfully proclaim the word of God. Preachers thus face a daunting task that requires such a respect for words that they will avoid words that are trite, tired, or tedious. I also suggest that a preacher's words are enhanced if surrounded by the power of silence. In other words, preaching is arduous work!

I now move to respect for congregational listeners. As I do, I confess that though I do not think I treated those listening to my sermons as know-nothings, I did not consider them as fully as I ought—until I heard a sermon by the American preacher Fred Craddock titled "When the Roll Is Called Down Here."[12] I laughed and cried as he explored the lengthy list of names in Rom 16. Craddock helped me to appreciate Paul's humanity, his understanding of "church," and how powerful sermons that respect listeners can be. For years I preached, Bible in hand, telling people what I thought they needed to hear, but it was often God, me, and the Bible ganging up on them!

Craddock's book *As One Without Authority*, originally published in 1971, addressed the decline of North American preaching and called preachers to replace their deductive-propositional three-point sermons

---

9. Long, "Taking the Listeners Seriously," 49.
10. Willimon, "Baptismal Speech," 455.
11. Quoted in Long, "Taking the Listeners Seriously," 43.
12. Craddock, "When the Roll Is Called."

with sermons that invite listeners on a journey that will help them to reframe their human experience when held up to the light of the Bible. Instead of sharing finished sermons, preachers should respect listeners enough to allow them to think, feel, decide, and make their own conclusion to the sermon. Craddock's book *Preaching*, published in 1985, put it like this: Listeners should be given "room to accept the responsibility for their own believing and doing."[13] And who are the listeners? "They are the creatures of God, every one of them. In fact, they are the crowning achievement of God's creation, God's masterpieces . . . . Some of the listeners do not know this about themselves and others have forgotten."[14] Craddock's respect for listeners changed me.

Yet Craddock's asking how listeners will respond to or resist the gospel, or how their lives are to be correlated to the Bible, is too listener-centered for those for whom preaching heralds a gospel that comes from beyond human experience. As Karl Barth wrote, "If God himself wills to speak the truth, preachers are forbidden to interfere with any sciences or art of their own."[15] Some who think Craddock's focus on listeners suggests a lack of confidence in the gospel want preachers to let the gospel reveal its own relevance rather than seek a point of contact for the gospel within hearers. But as Tom Long says, preachers have always thought about how best to convey the gospel, even the New Testament writers: "The biblical writings still show evidence of considerable attention to rhetorical dynamics . . . . Biblical writers themselves were concerned, in other words, not only with what they were saying but also with how they were saying it."[16]

Nevertheless, Long argues that while Craddock's inductive, narrative, story-telling sermons delighted congregations, American congregations with low biblical literacy need preachers to teach basic Christianity. Though the experience of listeners should be respected, and preachers should stand with listeners and not always against them, neither preachers nor listeners generate the gospel, writes Long.[17] Joseph McLelland made this point sixty years ago. Thinking of the incarnation as Christ coming to us from God, as well as Christ coming to stand with us before God, McLelland suggests the same pattern for preaching: a preacher should identify with listeners

---

13. Craddock, *Preaching*, 25 and 39.
14. Craddock, *Preaching*, 88.
15. Barth, *Homiletics*, 48.
16. Long, *Witness of Preaching*, 28.
17. Long, "Taking the Listeners Seriously," 47–51.

but at the same time "recognize that his message is not identifiable with the standards and the assumptions of his hearers."[18]

That preachers need to respect a word from God that comes to us from beyond us brings me to respect for the Bible in the preaching ministry. Though almost all denominations formally respect the Bible, some preachers interpret it as they see fit, and others avoid it, complained James Smart in his 1970 book, *The Strange Silence of the Bible in the Church*. But for most of its history, the church has believed that it is the Bible, inspired by God, that authorizes preachers to preach. Accordingly, John Calvin wrote that the work of pastors is "to proclaim the Word of God so as to teach, admonish, exhort and reprove both in public and in private."[19] Though Calvin and the Protestant tradition rarely said how God inspired the Bible, they were sure that the Holy Spirit spoke God's truth through it.

Traditional respect for the Bible has been, over time, challenged by various movements—the eighteenth-century Enlightenment doubted its miracles, nineteenth-century Bible critics claimed that the Bible was neither historically reliable nor divinely inspired, and Charles Darwin's 1859 publishing of *On the Origins of the Species* pitted his theory of evolution against the traditional view that Genesis teaches a six-day creation. Ever since then, a chasm has divided the Bible's conservative defenders from its radical critics. While conservatives cling to B. B. Warfield, the Princeton theologian who proposed the "plenary inspiration and inerrancy of Scripture"[20] in the 1880s, liberals align with a scholar like James Barr, who wrote in 1973 that "the biblical tradition is an account of a human work. It is man's statement of his beliefs, the events he has experienced, the stories he has been told. . . . It is man who developed the biblical tradition and man who decided when it might be suitably fixed and made canonical."[21]

Barr's view that the Bible is a human work raises a serious question: By what authority do preachers preach if the Bible is merely a collection of human insights? As to Warfield's view that each word of the Bible is God-inspired and inerrant, while it may protect the Bible's divine origin, it restrains respect for the Bible's human and historical origins. More helpful to me is how the prolific scholar N. T. Wright thinks of the Bible as a collection

---

18. McLelland, *Understanding the Faith*, 43.
19. Quoted in Parker, *Portrait of Calvin*, 80.
20. Nicole, "Warfield, Benjamin Breckinridge," 391.
21. Quoted in Morris, *I Believe in Revelation*, 104.

of neither moral rules nor doctrinal propositions, but as one story that narrates the unfolding of God's mission to restore God's rule.

The Bible's story about God, says Wright, can be read as an unfinished five-act play. Act 1 is creation; act 2 is the fall; act 3 is Israel; act 4 is Jesus; act 5a is the church's ministry begun by Spirit-filled apostles. In this scenario, act 5b is the church's ongoing ministry, kept on track as the church immerses itself in the biblical characters, plots, and purposes of God's people articulated in acts 1, 2, 3, 4, and 5a: "Our task is to discover, through the Spirit and prayer the appropriate ways of improvising the script between the foundation events . . . and the complete coming of the Kingdom."[22] For me, Wright's approach to the Bible respects both its divine and human origins and offers a way to cross the twentieth century's modernist-fundamentalist chasm without diminishing the authority of the Bible. In what follows, I offer some ways of reading the Bible, garnered from Wright and others, that help me to respect the Bible:[23]

- Respect for the Bible acknowledges its claims to be inspired by God but also respects that the Bible reflects the thought and cultural assumptions of the ancient Near East. Though the Bible was written for us, it was not written to us.
- Respect for the Bible entails coming to terms with its diverse literary genres. This means that interpreting a book about Israel's monarchy like 1 Kings calls for a different approach to interpreting Jesus' parables.
- Respect for the Bible means confessing that we don't fully know how it came to be—the origins for the Pentateuch, for example. Nor do we know for sure if the book of Job is the history of a man called Job or a "once upon a time" epic tale about a man called Job.
- Respect for the Bible is enhanced when we grasp that its trajectories reveal shifts in how some issues are understood within the Bible. For example, the place of women in the patriarchal culture reflected in the Old Testament radically changes in the New Testament.
- Respect for the Bible calls us to reckon with both continuity and discontinuity between Old and New Testaments and getting that balance

---

22. Wright, *Scripture and the Authority*, 126–27. For a resource to help congregations grasp Wright's reading of the Bible, see Goheen and Bartholomew, *True Story of the Whole World*.

23. *Living Faith*, a contemporary confession of faith for the Presbyterian Church in Canada, has a helpful chapter on the Bible.

- right. For example, God's law, a key concern in the Old Testament, changes in the New, but does not disappear.
- Respect for the Bible recognizes that its purpose isn't literary, scientific, or primarily historical. Its purpose, says the Westminster Confession of Faith, is to provide "that knowledge of God, and of his will, which is necessary unto salvation."[24]
- Respect for the Bible, given its ancient origins, its diversity of styles, and its theological purposes, will prevent us from imposing contemporary textbook precision on it.
- Respect for the Bible, most importantly, encourages us to read it as a drama that, as Bernard Anderson writes, works out "God's purpose for the creation in spite of all efforts to oppose it. The denouement is reached . . . when the crucifixion and resurrection of Jesus of Nazareth are proclaimed as the sign of God's decisive victory."[25]

Now to respect for God's role and that of preachers in the preaching ministry. It was long assumed that, given the Bible's divine inspiration, the primary task of Protestant preachers was to preach it. Calvin, who did much to shape Protestant ministry, imagines preachers as ambassadors with an authority that is borrowed, since ambassadors do not deliver their own message but that of the power they represent. But if it is God's word that witnesses to God's Son, and God's Spirit who enables God's Son to be heard, preachers do matter. T. H. L. Parker notes that Calvin used "the most definite language to assert that the preaching of the gospel is . . . as if the congregation 'heard the very words pronounced by God himself.' A man 'preaches so that God may speak to us by the mouth of a man.'"[26] Yes, preachers are to be modest, but they also have a dignity, because called, equipped, and sent as ambassadors to represent a sovereign God. For Craddock, "the person of the preacher is a vital element in effective preaching."[27] Because the gifts, graces, and personality of a preacher cannot be bleached out of the preaching ministry, the New Testament does not try to disguise the color, unique experiences, or personalities of Jesus's apostles.

If it is inappropriate for preachers to disappear, it is equally inappropriate for preachers to encourage a personality cult. Consider Henry

---

24. Quoted in *Our Confessional Heritage*, 85.
25. Anderson, *Unfolding Drama of the Bible*, 13.
26. Parker, *John Calvin*, 107.
27. Craddock, *Preaching*, 27.

Ward Beecher, the once famous pastor of Plymouth Church, Brooklyn, New York. In an 1871 lecture at Yale, Beecher stated that a "preacher is in some degree a reproduction of the truth in personal form.... The word of God in the book is a dead letter. It is paper, type, and ink. In the preacher that word becomes again as it was when first spoken by prophet, priest, or apostle."[28] So important did Beecher believe the personality of the preacher to be that he had Plymouth Church's sanctuary reconfigured to lessen the distance between him and his listeners. He reasoned: "A preacher must be a man among men. There is a force—call it magnetism, or electricity, or what you will—in a man, which is a personal element, and which flows from a speaker who is *en rapport* with his audience . . . I want them to surround me, so that they will come up on every side, and behind me, so that I shall be in the center of the crowd."[29]

The danger of a preacher-centric focus is obvious. In congregations of all sizes, preachers are tempted to use the pulpit for self-serving purposes; in doing so, they disrespect preaching and damage congregations. Jesus's famous words in Mark 8:34—"If any want to become my followers, let them deny themselves and take up their cross and follow me"—call his followers, and his preachers in particular, to die to their own advancement, agenda, and ambitions.

I commend Calvin's image of the preacher as ambassador as a wise one; while it respects the role of the preacher, it maintains that a preacher serves at the pleasure of another, operates under the authority of another, represents the interests of another, obeys the agenda of another, and is willing to be inconvenienced for the sake of another. Though preachers can help to build gathered congregations and equip them to scatter in God's service, they as servants of the word must die to self and place their confidence in a God who speaks. John Stott, describing God as living, redeeming, and self-revealing, writes,

> We should never presume to occupy a pulpit unless we believe in this God. How dare we speak if God has not spoken? By ourselves we have nothing to say. To address a congregation without any assurance that we are bearers of a divine message would be the height of arrogance and folly. It is when we are convinced that God is light [and so wanting to be known], that God has acted [and thus made

---

28. Beecher, *Yale Lectures on Preaching*, 3.
29. Beecher, *Yale Lectures on Preaching*, 72–73.

himself known], and that God has spoken [and thus explained his actions], that we must speak and cannot remain silent.[30]

I now turn to reflect on some aspects of worship that deserve respect if a gathered congregation is to grasp its christological identity and be equipped for missional witness. First this: Corporate worship that sets out to form and transform a gathered congregation will respect the need for preparation. I recall meeting a member of one congregation who told me that her minister's way of respecting the congregation was by always being well prepared. Consider seemingly mundane issues such as maximizing parking for worshipers; ensuring good signage outside and inside church buildings; the cleaning, heating, or cooling of said buildings; teaching worship greeters and ushers to understand their ministry as hospitality; or creating bulletins that do not have announcements like this: "To attend the PW meeting on Tuesday at 7:00, talk to Mary after worship, or just show up." What motivates thorough preparation (much of which is hidden) is respect for the capacity of corporate worship to enable people to encounter God and have their need for hope, meaning, forgiveness, transcendence, and more met. While it is true that a sovereign God is free to act beyond or in spite of human plans and preparation, that does not justify incoherent, underprepared corporate worship.

Respect for congregational worship also means understanding that it is public. The Bible rightly encourages private worship and prayer, not least by telling how Jesus retreated from the public to pray in private (see Mark 1:35, 6:46, 14:32–36); nevertheless, the New Testament gives greater attention to public congregational worship. In chapter 2, I noted how seriously the apostle Paul treated issues related to the worship of Corinth's congregation. He did this for one reason: Public worship is about encountering the true God and being formed as an "in Christ" community. Indeed, gathering for public worship is implicit in the word *ekklesia*, which means a public gathering, and is explicit in Heb 10:25, which tells believers to "consider how to provoke one another to love and good deeds, not neglecting to meet together."

But public worship is about more than congregations gathering publicly. First Corinthians 14 notes that Paul was so eager to have "outsiders" attend Corinth's congregational worship that he advised the congregation to accommodate outsiders by setting limits to speaking in tongues during worship (1 Cor 14:13–17). Convinced that the gospel is public truth, Paul wanted others to hear it, certainly as believers scattered to witness to Jesus, but also as

---

30. Stott, *I Believe in Preaching*, 96.

outsiders joined the worship gatherings of believers. So, while the New Testament distinguishes between worship and witness, it does not separate them.

As to the purpose of congregational worship, both the Old and New Testaments repeatedly encourage gatherings for worship that focus on praise for God, the Psalms in particular. In the New Testament, consider Heb 10:19–22, "Since we have confidence to enter the sanctuary by the blood of Jesus . . . let us approach with a true heart"; consider Eph 5:19, "be filled with the Spirit, as you sing psalms, and hymns and spiritual songs among yourselves, singing and making melody to the Lord"; and consider the vision of the ultimate worship gathering in Rev 5, when angels will sing, "Worthy is the Lamb that was slaughtered to receive power and wealth and wisdom and might and honor and glory and blessing," and "every creature in heaven and earth" will sing, "To the one seated on the throne and to the Lamb be blessing and honor and glory and might forever and ever!"

Yet those who gather to worship and praise the living God are themselves blessed, and congregations are built up. I quote Paul's words from 1 Cor 14:26: "When you come together, each one has a hymn, a lesson, a revelation, a tongue, or an interpretation. Let all things be done for building up." Paul uses the Greek word translated as "building up" six times in that chapter, so sure was he that worship builds and unifies congregations, no matter how challenging their social or ethnic diversity. Because worship gatherings have such community-building potential, Marva Dawn urges congregations to ensure that strangers are welcomed, that all are enabled to participate, and that worship is "kept open as a 'public space' into which every person can enter, rather than becoming the private coziness of individuals in their devotional relationship to God."[31]

Respect for congregational worship, then, means being clear that worship is about both God's praise and the building up of God's people. North American congregations know this, but they do not invariably respect what they know. For decades, conflict over worship style has so consumed congregations that respect for worship that praises God and builds up God's people is diminished. It is true that the New Testament does not prescribe a liturgy for congregations, but it does offer insights as to why and how apostolic congregations worshiped. Ralph Martin writes that they "entered into the inheritance of an already existing pattern of worship provided by the Temple ritual and synagogue Liturgy,"[32] adopting praise, prayer, and the

---

31. Dawn, *Royal "Waste" of Time*, 181.
32. Martin, *Worship in the Early Church*, 19.

reading and exposition of scripture from synagogue patterns, to which they added baptism and the Lord's Supper. But as to worship style or order, the New Testament is largely silent.

During the 1960s, unease with the traditional worship of North America's congregations deepened. At the same time, new forms of worship appeared within charismatic, Catholic, and avant-garde Christian circles. Since then, those eager to retain the liturgical riches of the past tend to dismiss the new forms, while those eager to connect congregations to contemporary culture tend to dismiss tradition. Bill Easum claimed that the Christian message "remains the same, but the package in which the message is conveyed is conditioned by the culture of the times," and told congregations to ditch traditional music, since "every survey will show that 'soft rock' is the music of the majority of unchurched people in America."[33] If people complain, it is a signal, says Easum, that "their love of music rivals their love of Christ."[34] On the other hand, John Bell, a Scottish worship leader who values both older and newer worship forms, dismisses a swath of American contemporary worship songs as "white Protestant trash."[35]

Conflict about worship, particularly about what congregations sing, is often a battle over personal preferences and ought to raise this question: What helps gathered congregations to praise God and be formed as God's people? Before addressing that, I suggest that if some contemporary worship songs are dubious, the same is true of some traditional songs and hymns. As a Sunday school kid sixty years ago, I sang "I Am H-A-P-P-Y," "I'm Too Young to March with the Infantry," and "Climb, Climb Up Sunshine Mountain"; in church I sang hymns that included the following verses:

> By cool Siloam's shady rill
> How sweet the lily grows!
> How sweet the breath, beneath the hill,
> Of Sharon's dewy rose!
>
> Days and moments quickly flying
> Blend the living with the dead;
> Soon will you and I be lying
> Each within his narrow bed.

---

33. Easum, *Dancing with Dinosaurs*, 84.
34. Easum, *Dancing with Dinosaurs*, 88.
35. Bell, "Reforming Worship," 9.

> Joy-bells ringing, children singing,
> Fill the air with music sweet;
> Joyful measure, guileless pleasure,
> Make the chain of song complete.
> Joy-bells! Joy-bells! Never, never cease your ringing;
> Children! Children! Never, never cease your singing;
> List, list the song that swells, Joy-bells! joy-bells![36]

Clearly, some eighteenth- and nineteenth-century hymns are as theologically thin as some contemporary hymns and songs, and many are no longer sung. Of Charles Wesley's six thousand hymns, congregations now sing only a few dozen. So, the key issue around what congregations sing isn't how old or new their hymns or songs are, but whether they do justice to God's character and have the capacity to form congregations that serve God's mission. "Instead of asking what kind of music will appeal to the world around us," writes Marva Dawn in *A Royal "Waste" of Time*, we should ask what "will enable us most deeply to dwell in God's Word? What will best express that Word? How will the Word's beauty and mystery, its infinity and generosity be best conveyed?"[37]

Thinking of worship songs, I must mention Nick Page's hilarious book, *And Now Let's Move into a Time of Nonsense*. Page, a contemporary worship songwriter, reveals how charismatic renewal on both sides of the Atlantic during the 1970s gave birth to an explosion of guitar-led, emotion-filled worship songs that quickly came to constitute what worship is in charismatic and renewal church circles. He notes that those worship songs appealed to the feelings of worshipers, but not to their thinking, and adds, "if the words aren't giving us any deep truth, then the emotion is all we've got."[38] Page concludes that while worship songs encourage intimate, individualistic worship and a "buzz," they often turn congregational worship into a pop concert performance.

What worries Nick Page, John Bell, and others about contemporary worship songs is their limited theology—the overuse of a few biblical images and their inattention to Jesus's earthly life, the Old Testament, and the Trinity. Bell also notes that "the tendency in contemporary music writing is for composers to write out of their own experience and for their own voice

---

36. Verses found at nos. 787, 609, and 774 in Presbyterian Church in Canada, *Book of Praise*.

37. Dawn, *Royal "Waste" of Time*, 15.

38. Page, *And Now Let's Move*, 31.

and fingers, not thinking about the people who will be singing the words. In doing so, they miss the target. All of God's people are asked to sing a new song. And if a church musician doesn't respect the congregation in the first place, then that's not going to happen."[39]

If one cause of worship disrespect is conflict over contemporary Christian songs, another is forgetfulness over what Christian worship is. Most congregations know that worship is meant to focus on God and God's praise, yet some congregational leaders allow congregational worship to be hijacked to serve other agendas. I once wrote an article in the monthly magazine of my denomination that complained about how many Sundays were being designated to special causes by the denomination, causes that clergy were then to promote in their congregation's worship services, using promotional material provided by denominational agencies. Clergy, of course, pick which and to what extent they will promote specially designated Sundays, whether Healing and Reconciliation Sunday, Presbyterians Sharing Sunday, Christian Family Sunday, Legacy Giving Sunday, Earth Day Sunday, Heritage Sunday, and so on. Now, if a mission moment or prayer is devoted to a special cause, fine; but what can happen is that clergy, especially if they are deferential to denominational agencies, may end up building Sunday worship around various causes and making them the "topic" of their sermons.

I am not at all objecting to fine causes, but to the fact that, cumulatively, their promotion in Sunday worship can hijack worship by diluting its potential to be an encounter between God's word and God's people. It is right that Christians, anxious to see the church respond to a range of world problems, want God to help, but the danger, writes Donald McCullough, is that "instead of serving God by working for a just cause, we serve a just cause by using God. The cause pushes God aside; the divine end becomes simply a useful means, and God gets trivialized."[40] For example, in the 2018 Advent liturgies, designed by my denomination to support the excellent work of Presbyterian World Service and Development and to be used during congregational worship, the name of Jesus did not appear, though the title Christ did in the Christmas Eve liturgy. In essence, those liturgies pushed Jesus aside. I suspect that some North American congregations, more ready to act than pray, and aware that society considers worship "a

---

39. Bell, "Reforming Worship," 9.
40. McCullough, *Trivialization of God*, 28.

royal waste of time," hope that, if used to harness support for refugees or fighting poverty, worship will justify itself.

Marva Dawn strenuously challenges using worship for utilitarian ends. Though worship has evangelistic capacity, allows friends to enjoy being together, and can support worthy causes, worship, she argues, is essentially about encountering God through God's word. Read and taught in worship, scripture meets "our genuine needs for repentant insight, constant forgiveness, authentic security, unconditional love, absolute healing, faithful presence, fruitful freedom, compelling motivation and coherent guidance for daily life, and eternal hope."[41] Dawn adds that the scriptures "form us to react as God's people with kingdom values to the problems and social issues of our everyday lives."[42] Worship, while centered on God's truth, holiness, love, grace, and saving power, does not remove believers from life's challenges but prepares them to address them. Dawn ends *A Royal "Waste" of Time* by telling worshiping congregations to give the world

> true hope that is not entertainment, nor escapism, nor diversion, nor a consumerist appeal to taste, but that teaches us instead a realistic appraisal of sin and evil, that reminds us of the victory of Christ over sin and evil at the cross and empty tomb, that enfolds us in the presence of God's reign in the world now, that challenges us to participate in that reign in ministry to our world, and that assures us of the truth that someday God will usher in his kingdom in all its fullness.[43]

Given the confusion and conflict over worship within North American congregations in recent decades, the question must be asked: What is it that gives Christian worship its integrity? In 1971, the same year that Fred Craddock published *As One Without Authority*, Paul Hoon, a professor at Union Seminary, New York, published *The Integrity of Worship*. Like Craddock, Hoon addressed the impact of the 1960s cultural revolution on American congregations, noting the penchant then for new worship forms. Hoon describes "a Protestant jazz service at which dancers moved through the aisles hurling paper plates at the congregation bearing newspaper advertisements and biblical texts"[44] and then asks the question: What gives worship its integrity?

41. Dawn, *Royal "Waste" of Time*, 67–68.
42. Dawn, *Royal "Waste" of Time*, 69.
43. Dawn, *Royal "Waste" of Time*, 370.
44. Hoon, *Integrity of Worship*, 25.

The question of what sustains the integrity of worship is closely related to my concern that the power of worship to form and inspire a gathered congregation be respected. Most of us have been present at a worship service where respect for its practical preparation was missing, where respect for the public nature of Christian worship was replaced by a sense that we were in the midst of a private meeting for old friends, where the liturgy was disrespected by being incoherent or, much worse, that the focus of the worship service was not on God, who it seemed, was not even expected to show up. So, what is it, asks Hoon, that gives Christian worship its integrity?

Addressing the fallout from the 1960s cultural revolution, Hoon was aware of the pressure to make worship serve useful ends such as raising the budget, winning new converts, building good citizens, or changing the world; aware of those who wanted to dignify Protestant worship by using colored stoles and fastidious liturgies; and aware of social activists who demanded that worship be socially relevant. Though empathetic to such concerns since worship must connect with the whole of life, Hoon wrote that "the center of gravity for liturgical reflection and decision must always remain God, the End beyond all other ends."[45] He reached this conclusion after asking what relevance, theology, tradition, and the church contribute to worship's integrity.

As to relevance, Hoon noted the contradiction between "well-filled churches on Sunday and the immoralities of our society" and that the impact of American congregations on American society was weak. Yet Hoon warned that "worship can lose its integrity when it is regarded as a means to something else—even to the moral end of social action,"[46] and that to play off Christian service in the world against Christian worship in sanctuaries contradicts the New Testament's concern that believers both serve the world and gather for worship.

As to theology, it has the power to shape worship and correct its distortions. Yet worship, Hoon argues, precedes theological reflection and may correct theology from time to time; here, he refers to Oscar Cullmann's point that the "great perception that Jesus rules as the present Lord over his church . . . was given to the first Christians in common worship."[47] As to tradition, Hoon notes its positive value in relaying the mind of the church universal, reminding us that the church never worships "*de novo*," and that

---

45. Hoon, *Integrity of Worship*, 54.
46. Hoon, *Integrity of Worship*, 30–31.
47. Hoon, *Integrity of Worship*, 90.

the "Spirit is as much the source of continuity, of order, and of heritage as it is of newness and freedom."[48] But though tradition can help to sustain worship's integrity, it is not decisive, because the "heart of worship is not tradition; it is Jesus Christ encountering the human soul."[49]

As to the church, it preserves worship's integrity by sustaining its apostolic pattern of Word and Sacraments and its corporate nature, such that to absent oneself from worship "does not so much 'let the pastor down' as deal a wound to the Christian community."[50] Yet, says Hoon, "worship is finally determined not by the Church but by the . . . Lord of the Church . . . the church as Christ's body is not identical with Christ."[51]

Hoon circles back to his basic claim that the character of worship is largely determined by the trinitarian character of God. Yet Hoon insists that the development of trinitarian doctrine was preceded by the lived experience of Jesus's first disciples who, after spending years with Jesus, were convinced that he was the Messiah, and were further convinced that, having risen from the dead, Jesus was God's Son who, ascended to the Father, was present to them through the Holy Spirit. Hoon writes: "As it was the encounter with Jesus Christ . . . which originally inspired the doctrine of the Trinity, so the decisive center of liturgical theology lies not in the Trinity in general but in Jesus Christ in particular."[52] Worship's integrity rests on a Christology that ties believing congregations to the scandal of particularity: Jesus.

I appreciate Paul Hoon's book *The Integrity of Worship* because it taught me respect for worship and answers a key question: What is worship's purpose? Hoon's answer is that those who trust the God who sent Jesus to seek sinners and call them into a new life gather to worship God and have God's word change their thinking, affections, morals, and hopes, such that they are formed to serve God's mission. For Hoon, it is Jesus who finally guarantees the integrity of Christian worship: "God has acted to save man in a way in which he could not save himself—in the calling of Israel to be his people . . . and supremely in the Event of Jesus Christ in which all other acts of God are summed up. This historical matrix of salvation history is decisive for worship."[53]

48. Hoon, *Integrity of Worship*, 97–98.
49. Hoon, *Integrity of Worship*, 101.
50. Hoon, *Integrity of Worship*, 106.
51. Hoon, *Integrity of Worship*, 113.
52. Hoon, *Integrity of Worship*, 115.
53. Hoon, *Integrity of Worship*, 135.

Respecting Congregations

Paul Hoon's concern that Jesus's centrality in Christian worship be respected is echoed in the Scottish theologian James Torrance's book *Worship, Community, and the Triune God of Grace*, published a generation after Hoon. Torrance begins with a lament:

> Probably the most common and widespread view is that worship is something which we, religious people do . . . . We go to church, we sing our psalms and hymns to God, we intercede for the world, we listen to the sermon . . . we offer our money, time and talents to God . . . . We sit in the pew watching the minister "doing his thing," exhorting us "to do our thing," until we go home thinking we have done our duty for another week.[54]

Such worship, says Torrance, is tiring, unitarian, individualistic, and moralistic, and it pays little or no attention to Jesus Christ as the mediator of worship. By way of contrast, Torrance appreciates how the Letter to the Hebrews presents Jesus not only as the mediator of revelation through whom God "has spoken to us" (Heb 1:2), and as the mediator of redemption through whose death God destroyed "the one who has the power of death, that is, the devil" (Heb 2:14), but presents Jesus as the ascended mediator through whom our worship is brought to God. As Heb 10:19 says, "we have confidence to enter the sanctuary by the blood of Jesus." Christian worship is essentially, writes Torrance, "our participation through the Spirit in the Son's communion with the Father."[55]

The Letter to the Hebrews also teaches that there is more going on when a congregation gathers for worship than we imagine; for flawed congregations join the worship of "innumerable angels" and the saints already "enrolled in heaven" when they gather to worship God through "Jesus, the mediator" (Heb 12:22-24). Congregations gathered for worship are being readied for their scattered ministry on earth, but they are also rehearsing for the day when God will make "all things new" (Rev 21:5). Respect for the gathered worship of congregations keeps together the ancient church liturgy: Christ has died, Christ is risen, Christ will come again.

As I end this section, I note that not all congregations respect gathered ministries. On the one hand, some evangelical clergy neglect to build up their congregations through preaching and worship, instead using their congregations as a base from which to launch evangelistic ministry beyond

---

54. Torrance, *Worship, Community, and the Triune*, 20.
55. Torrance, *Worship, Community, and the Triune*, 15.

the congregation. Evangelism is indeed a vital ministry, but not to the neglect of gathered congregational ministry.

On the other hand, some liberal clergy neglect to build up their congregations through preaching and worship in order to pursue kingdom ministry beyond their congregations. P. T. Forsyth, an early twentieth-century British theologian, wrote in 1907 about "impatient reformers" who speak of "the edification of believers as a mere "coddling of the Saints," and who pressure clergy "to go straight to the world" rather than bother with gathered congregations.[56] Forsyth's response was that it is congregations, edified by the preaching and teaching of Christ, that are to go to the world: "The genius of the Gospel is after all best understood by the personal believers in the gospel. And that genius certainly is to go to the world ... through the ... common action of believing men, who are mature enough ... to be sure, without cavil, that their Gospel is the tragic, desperate world's one hope."[57] Encouraged by Forsyth, I move on to the scattered part of the ministry pattern of New Testament congregations.

RESPECTING THE SCATTERED MINISTRY OF CONGREGATIONS

North American Christians have long thought of God's mission as based on the Great Commission of Matt 28—"Jesus came and said to them, 'All authority in heaven and earth has been given to me. Go therefore and make disciples of all nations, baptizing them in the name of the Father and of the Son and of the Holy Spirit'" (Matt 28:18–19). That commission, used for centuries to recruit people to serve as overseas missionaries, is rarely linked to the local ministry of North American congregations. As a result, the idea that congregations are to scatter to serve God's mission is unfamiliar to them, and they fulfill any sense they have of the call to mission contained in the Great Commission by sending annual checks to a few favored mission agencies.

Yet the idea that a congregation is itself a local mission agency for God is not as rare as it once was, thanks to the missional theologians. I think of Christopher Wright's book *The Mission of God's People*, quoted in chapter 4. It reminds us that God's original mission was for God's people to care for creation (Gen 1), but given the rebellion of humans against their creator and the tragic escalation of sin and evil that follows (Gen 3–11),

---

56. Forsyth, *Positive Preaching*, 75–77.
57. Forsyth, *Positive Preaching*, 78–79.

Respecting Congregations

God's mission now focuses on replacing the curse of sin and evil with blessing. This mission in which congregations are to participate, Wright points out, began with God's promise to Abraham—"I will make of you a great nation, and I will bless you, and make your name great, so that you will be a blessing . . . and in you all the families of the earth shall be blessed" (Gen 12:2–3). Wright traces this mission through the Old and New Testaments as one of "the key unifying threads in the whole Bible,"[58] and notes that if Abraham's family Israel was chosen to carry forward God's mission, all nations will be its beneficiaries.

As to who now constitutes Abraham's family, Wright refers to Rom 4:16–17; there Paul clarifies that "people of any and every nation who believe in Jesus as Messiah and saviour are included in the seed of Abraham and are inheritors of the promise made to Abraham . . . if we are in Christ, we not only share in the blessing of Abraham; we are commissioned to spread the blessing of Abraham."[59] The church, made up of Jews and gentiles who believe that Jesus's death "redeemed us from the curse" (Gal 3:13), is a community of blessing that, to use George Hunsberger's words, is to "represent God's reign as its community, its servant, and its messenger."[60]

My point, and Wright's, is that congregational scattered ministry rests not only on the Great Commission but on a missional reading of the whole Bible. If the Old Testament sees Israel as called to draw all nations to Israel's God, the New Testament sees the church as called to scatter to all the nations with the good news of Jesus. It is, of course, much cozier for Christians to gather for a Bible study or a men's breakfast or to make prayer shawls than it is to contemplate leaving such fellowship gatherings to engage in scattered ministry. But they must attempt it if they are to respect the New Testament's pattern of congregations gathering and then scattering, the latter appearing in a text such as Col 4:6, where Paul advises the congregation in Colossae: "Conduct yourselves wisely toward outsiders, making the most of the time. Let your speech always be gracious, seasoned with salt, so that you may know how you ought to answer everyone."

For most believers, the New Testament's call for gathered congregations to also scatter means doing so in their own neighborhoods. First Peter 3:8–16 highlights this responsibility:

---

58. Wright, *Mission of God's People*, 71.
59. Wright, *Mission of God's People*, 72.
60. Hunsberger, "Missional Vocation," 102.

Respecting Congregational Ministry

> Finally, all of you, have unity of spirit, sympathy, love for one another, a tender heart, and a humble mind. Do not repay evil for evil or abuse for abuse; but, on the contrary, repay with a blessing. It is for this that you were called—that you might inherit a blessing....
>
> Now who will harm you if you are eager to do what is good? But even if you do suffer for doing what is right, you are blessed. Do not fear what they fear, and do not be intimidated, but in your hearts sanctify Christ as Lord. Always be ready to make your defense to anyone who demands from you an account of the hope that is in you; yet do it with gentleness and reverence. Keep your conscience clear, so that, when you are maligned, those who abuse you for your good conduct in Christ may be put to shame.

This advice, given to encourage congregations living in a hostile environment to persevere with their scattered ministry, uses the word "blessing" twice and the word "blessed" once, words that echo Jesus's Beatitudes and God's ancient promise to bless the nations through Abraham. Even at the best of times, congregations find it hard to have a "unity of spirit, sympathy, love for one another, a tender heart, and a humble mind" (1 Pet 3:8), but Peter expects much more from the congregations to whom he writes that he refers to as the "exiles of the Dispersion in Pontus, Galatia, Cappadocia, Asia, and Bithynia" (1 Pet 1:1); namely, the apostle expects that when enemies insult and malign communities of believers, they will not "repay evil for evil or abuse for abuse; but, on the contrary, repay with a blessing"(1 Pet 3:9).

How should congregations engage a North American society that is suspicious of them rather than hostile toward them? Many of them are tempted to choose one of the following:

1. Anger. During the Christendom era, congregations in Canada and the USA were given unquestioned support within their nations. That has changed, leaving Christians who still attend church feeling angry toward a society that seems indifferent to them, or worse. I hear that anger in believers who are baffled that Canada's schools no longer allow the Lord's Prayer. Less frequent in Canada than in the US, some congregations engage in angry cultural wars to fight their secular enemies. First Peter 3 offers them no support, for it urges congregations to conduct their scattered ministry with "gentleness and reverence" (1 Pet 3:16)—the word "reverence" being translated in both the New English Bible and the New International Version of the Bible as "respect."

2. Abandonment. Some congregations, aware of their diminished status in society, choose to withdraw from it and in essence hide. Feeling intimidated by the society in which they live, such congregations abandon any local scattered mission and operate as a private group, even if ready to support faraway Christian missions. Again, 1 Pet 3 offers little support; to the contrary, verses 13–14 urge congregations facing determined hostility on a scale unknown to North American congregations not to fear or be intimidated but to be ready to "suffer for doing what is right."

3. Accommodation. For a long time, North America publicly endorsed the Christian faith. That is no longer the case, making it difficult for churches to hold and promote Christian values discarded by our society. Feeling misunderstood by mainstream society, some congregations try to minimize what differentiates them from that society. I noted earlier the hesitancy of some mainline churches to publicly name Jesus, a hesitancy that discourages such congregations from engaging in a scattered ministry that witnesses to Jesus. However, 1 Pet 3:15 tells first-century congregations to "always be ready to make your defense to anyone who demands from you an accounting for the hope that is in you."

It is worth noting that the apostle Peter's call for intimidated Christian congregations to witness to Jesus within alien environments by speaking and acting with "gentleness and reverence" (1 Pet 3:16) echoes how the prophet Jeremiah centuries earlier called Jewish exiles living in Babylon to speak and act: "Seek the welfare of the city where I have sent you into exile, and pray to the Lord on its behalf, for in its welfare you will find your welfare" (Jer 29:7). Rather than being angry with, abandoning, or accommodating the society in which it lives, a Christian congregation, aware of God's plan to bring blessing to the world, will understand that it has a mission within its local community that is to be marked, not by belligerence, but by respect and an eagerness "to do what is good" (1 Pet 3:13). Given that the apostle Peter refers to Christ's "leaving you an example, so that you should follow in his steps" (1 Pet 2:21), it is likely that as Peter tells congregations to witness to Christ with "gentleness and reverence," he still has Christ in mind, the Christ whom the Gospels portray as being judicious and respectful, but also open to turning his enemies into his friends.

Respecting Congregational Ministry

To help congregations to respect and then engage in scattered ministry, I suggest two approaches. The first takes seriously the scale of God's global mission. Acts 1:8 tells how the risen Jesus promised the Holy Spirit to enable his disciples to "be my witnesses in Jerusalem, in all Judea and Samaria, and to the ends of the earth." Acts 9:30 tells how Jerusalem's believers sent Paul to Tarsus, Acts 11:22 tells how "the church in Jerusalem . . . sent Barnabas to Antioch," and Acts 13:1 tells how "the church in Antioch" later "laid their hands on [Barnabas and Paul] and sent them off" to serve God's mission even further afield. From the beginning, the church has had a sending, scattering mission. I first became aware of that mission when, as a boy, I accompanied my aunt as she visited homes seeking support for the Leprosy Mission. That awareness deepened when my high school in Northern Ireland, though not formally Christian, raised funds to provide bicycles for missionaries serving in Malawi. Slowly, it dawned on me that ordinary Christians are called to share and support God's promise to bless the world.

Congregations that respect their call to serve God's ongoing global mission will find ways to get to know, connect to, pray for, and participate in the scattered ministry of the worldwide church. Here are some practical suggestions for congregational leaders:

1. Invite congregants to read or to together study Philip Jenkins's 2002 book, *The Next Christendom: The Coming of Global Christianity*, which I quoted in chapter 3. It presents a broad picture of the global church that is both challenging and exciting.

2. Ensure that congregations receive educational material about the global ministries of their denomination. Not all local believers can travel across the globe, but they can learn a good deal about the global church and the people from their own ranks who serve overseas. Use bulletin inserts to inform congregations about specific countries, projects, and people, and follow up with prayer for those ministries and missions.

3. Encourage congregants to identify places around the globe where they have some connection, and from there develop global partnerships. Such partnerships are more and more possible using internet technology. In one congregation I served, a couple who had served in Malawi as a doctor and nurse brought our congregation's attention to that country's need for doctors. The congregation responded by financing

the full six-year medical education of a young Malawian woman, whom we were able to occasionally meet online.

4. Encourage congregants to attend worship when holidaying abroad, and to bring the greetings of their home congregation to the congregation being visited. Interacting with Christians across the globe makes real the church's oneness. At the same time, our congregations can welcome Christians from abroad, and from time to time also invite those serving God abroad to share their challenges and joys in person.

5. Support a specialized agency that scatters the gospel, maybe one already supported by a congregational member—a farmer who supports the ministry of the Canadian Foodgrains Bank, a pilot who is excited to support the Mission Aviation Fellowship, or a French teacher who is intrigued by Wycliffe Bible Translators. I think of my late brother Alan, who, during his academic career teaching engineering at the University of Glasgow, became a consultant on water management to various governments in Africa. As a committed Christian, he later offered his engineering expertise to a British Christian charity then developing hundreds of village wells in Malawi, one of the poorest countries on the planet. In this process, Alan, his life and faith formed in gathered congregations, engaged the interest, prayers, and financial support of the congregation to which he belonged and many others, in the ministry of gospel scattering.

Having addressed how congregations can engage in scattered ministry that is geographically distant from them, I now suggest a second approach to scattered ministry that takes seriously a congregation's role in God's mission within its local community. If a congregation is a body of believers that gathers to become more Christ-like through preaching, worship, prayer, and more, it is also a body of believers called to locally embody, exhibit, and express something of the kingdom of God. There is a time to gather as a congregation but also a time to scatter and live as Christ's witnesses in local neighborhoods, among family, friends, work colleagues, other residents, and strangers. The most frequent form of neighborhood ministry in which congregations engage is social in nature—feeding, housing, clothing, or advocating for those in need. Such scattering is legitimate, for it seeks to do what Jesus told us to do—"love your neighbor."

A useful resource to help congregations engage in neighborhood ministry is Mark Mulder's book *Congregations, Neighborhoods, Places*. Mulder is aware of the challenge of such ministry and the temptations that lead congregations to avoid it. If some larger regional congregations encourage members to drive significant distances to attend worship, and so bypass the messy particularities of local neighborhoods on the way, other congregations, keen to engage their local neighborhood, find themselves discouraged by the human needs they encounter and quickly give up. Congregations serve best, writes Mulder, "when they complement existing social services—not when they seek to replace those programs."[61] That still leaves even small congregations with lots of opportunities to serve others, bringing, as Jesus did, "good news to the poor . . . release to the captives . . . sight to the blind . . . [and letting] the oppressed go free" (Luke 4:18).

Yet it must be said that scattered ministry raises some critical issues, especially if that ministry is based on compassion for the needy. First, ministry that addresses visible need often presents congregations as generous people who help recipients on the other side of a social divide. Second, doing such ministry may conceal the fact that its givers are as much in need of God's mercy as receivers. Third, ministry addressed to visible need may bypass neighbors whose need for God's love, forgiveness, new life, and lasting hope is less visible. Fourth, those active in "doing" ministries sometimes use their "doing" to exempt themselves from obeying 1 Pet 3:15–16—"be ready to make your defense to anyone who demands from you an accounting for the hope that is in you," a text that calls believers to verbally witness to Jesus "with gentleness and reverence." Though it is easier to exhibit faith in deeds than to express it in words, congregations ought to do both.

As to how a congregation might respect the New Testament's call to local scattered ministry, I turn to Alan Roxburgh's 2015 book, *Joining God, Remaking Church, Changing the World*, quoted in chapter 4. Roxburgh, a Canadian member of the GOCN, reviews the attempts over the last five decades to "fix" North American churches. These attempts, he says, have not reversed the numerical decline of the church. Roxburgh traces this failure at least in part to the fact that North America's clergy-led Euro-tribal churches are church-centered rather than God-centered. But if mission is God's initiative, argues Roxburgh, then God is the primary actor in mission, not the church; that should lead us to "assume God is already ahead of us" in local neighborhoods. If so, the "church's primary work is to listen for what God is already up to. Its life should be marked by listening, watching,

---

61. Mulder, *Congregations, Neighborhoods, Places*, 58.

entering, and participating in the life of the neighborhoods where God's people live in the ordinary and everyday, rather as Jesus did."[62]

As to congregations engaging with their neighborhoods, Roxburgh notes that contact with neighbors is discouraged by a car culture and highly privatized lives lived behind high fences and locked doors. Accordingly, he urges congregations to go to their neighborhoods and to simply listen, implying that it may be time for Christians to stop talking and to stop assuming that they have answers for all their neighbors' questions. Roxburgh's proposal that believers listen to each other, to God, and to neighbors reflects his critique of the schemes and strategies that North American congregations have pursued in recent decades in an attempt to stem their decline—a decline that the work of the missional theologians has not reversed. Roxburgh's proposal may be timely if it nudges mainline congregations toward reengaging their neighborhoods and encourages evangelistic congregations to speak less aggressively to their neighbors.

Roxburgh's call for congregations to listen respects the fact that the society in which we live suspects the church and offers another option to congregations tempted to respond to that society with anger, abandonment, or accommodation. But I wonder if Roxburgh is overreacting. *Joining God, Remaking Church, Changing the World* calls congregations to listen to and discuss what they discover about their neighbors, but does not go beyond that. Roxburgh may be right in wanting to temper the often injudicious attempts of congregations to "do mission"; nevertheless, the New Testament encourages congregations not only to listen respectfully to their neighbors but to walk worthily among them, and by word and deed to witness to Jesus. In *Called to Witness*, Darrell Guder quotes what Paul told Philippi's congregation: "Let your manner of life be worthy of the gospel of Christ, so that . . . I will know that you are standing firm in one spirit, striving side by side with one mind for the faith of the gospel, and are in no way intimidated by your opponents" (Phil 1:27–28). Paul's call for congregations to walk worthily, says Guder, "speaks of purposeful movement accompanied by distinctive conduct," and he quotes Stephen Fowl's comment that to walk worthily "entails that the members of the body display certain types of habits, dispositions, and practices toward one another . . . that demonstrate before a watching world what the inbreaking kingdom of God is really all about."[63]

---

62. Roxburgh, *Joining God, Remaking Church*, 43–44.
63. Guder, *Called to Witness*, 134–36.

Guder would no doubt endorse the idea that congregational scattered ministry involves carefully listening to neighbors, but he goes beyond that, hoping that the behavior of congregations will evangelistically impact their neighbors. Roxburgh would, I imagine, affirm Guder's proposal that congregations walk worthily as they scatter among their neighbors as parents, grandparents, teachers, shop assistants, accountants, or personal care workers.

As to evangelism that verbalizes faith to our neighbors, 1 Pet 3:15–16 ("Be ready to make your defense to anyone who demands from you an accounting for the hope that is in you") joins many New Testament texts in expecting not just apostles, evangelists, prophets, or preachers to "speak Jesus," but also ordinary believers. Little is known about how they did that in New Testament times. What we do know is that belief in Jesus's resurrection led thousands of people to risk confessing Christ and being publicly baptized, to create and then "sing psalms, hymns and spiritual songs to God" (Col 3:16), to generously support Christ's cause, and to gossip the gospel wherever they went, an activity that is explicit in Acts 8:4 and implicit in Phlm 1:6 and Eph 6:15.

As noted earlier, giving witness to Jesus to our neighbors is not easy, which is why most congregations prefer gathering to scattering. But if congregations are to respect the identity, purpose, and ministry pattern that the New Testament articulates for them, then the ministry of scattering must be attempted. To help with the latter, I commend a book by Canadian Anglican cleric Harold Percy, titled *Good News People: An Introduction to Evangelism for Tongue-Tied Christians*. Written for mainline congregations and now a generation old, the book invites the fearful followers of Jesus to respect the New Testament's call for congregations to scatter and to serve God's mission.

CONCLUSION

This chapter did not set out to offer homiletic or liturgical advice to congregational leaders or to tell them how to do outreach.[64] Its purpose has been to point out why and how congregations should respect the gathered/scattered pattern of congregational ministry that the New Testament outlines. For all sorts of reasons, respecting this pattern is difficult. One reason is that leaders of congregations now find themselves spending so much time and

---

64. I commend Harold Percy's book *Your Church Can Thrive*.

effort keeping their struggling congregations afloat; another is the constant and legitimate needs of congregants for pastoral care. There is also the fact that some clergy are tempted to at least one of the following: to whine, to recline, or to shine. All three of those temptations, if given into, inhibit the sort of discipline it takes to think big thoughts and to build congregations.

But perhaps the most serious obstacle that prevents congregational leaders from seriously examining their ministry priorities and practices is their fear of pain. That may sound odd, but it is true. To take time to examine what we do in any endeavor—and that includes leading a congregation—is to entertain the notion that we may not be doing what we ought to be doing, and to face the fact that change may be required. I recall how painful it was for me as an eight-year-old boy to change how I played the piano. Up to that point, I had taught myself to play, but then I was sent to a fine piano teacher who insisted, to my great displeasure, that I must set aside my way of playing and learn to play all over again. I still recall the pain of hurt pride!

Taking time to examine the effectiveness of the gathered ministry of preaching and worship in forming and transforming a congregation so that "it will grow up in every way into him who is the head, into Christ" (Eph 4:15), and taking time to rethink the effectiveness of the scattered ministry of a congregation so that its light shines "before others [who] see your good works and give glory to your Father in heaven" (Matt 5:16), is infinitely more important than relearning how to play a piano. God's desire to bless others and our desire that God receive glory will not remove the pain that congregational self-examination involves, but they ought to motivate it.

Epilogue

OTHER THAN SOME SECTIONS of chapter 5, my book has offered little in the way of hands-on practical help to congregations and their leaders. My purpose was otherwise: to press the idea that time taken from the pressures and problems of congregational life to rethink what a congregation is, why a congregation exists, and what a congregation's ministry pattern and priorities should be will turn out to be time well spent. More than that, I have argued that Christian congregations are not at liberty to set aside the three New Testament–based givens that define Christian congregations: their christological identity, their missional purpose, and their gathering/scattering ministry pattern. To respect these givens is not to forgo freedom but to find it, for true freedom comes to those who know who they are, why they are, and what they are called to do. Though congregations that have a quiet confidence that God has called them to serve Christ's kingdom are not guaranteed an easy life, they may well enjoy effective ministry outcomes. What I am getting at echoes the oft-quoted questions that Peter Drucker, the famous management consultant, asked America's corporations: "What business are you in?" and "How's business?"[1]

To illustrate the power that clarity of purpose offers, I share my own experience. After spending twenty years in congregational ministry, the General Assembly of the Presbyterian Church in Canada appointed me the director of pastoral studies at Presbyterian College, Montreal. At that small theological college, I wore many hats. On arrival, Principal John Vissers, perhaps more confident in my abilities than I was, asked me to teach a preaching course, a worship course, and a course on the Reformed tradition; to jointly teach a theology of ministry course; to be responsible for

1. Quoted in Robinson, *Transforming Congregational Culture*, 25.

Respecting Congregations

theological field education; to coordinate the college chapel; and to sort out student bursary needs. For two years, I did my best, but my best was not good. Frustrated by trying to keep multiple balls in the air at the same time, which is how many congregational leaders feel, I finally took the time to figure out what all the bits and pieces of my role amounted to. It was this: to help to form pastors. Those five words sound both simple and obvious, but it took me a good deal of time to arrive at the point where they articulated my college ministry and, in the process, helped me to relax enough to enjoy that ministry. As for clergy in congregations, based on the three major ways to respect a congregation I have urged, I suggest this summary for their ministry: to clarify that a congregation is a christological community located in a specific cultural context, and to edify a congregation using all the means of grace, such that the congregation's internal life and external words and deeds witness to Jesus Christ, through whom God is restoring God's kingdom—on earth as it is in heaven.

But here's the thing: Congregational leaders do not have the luxury of stepping away from their daily responsibilities while they take time to rethink and reframe the identity, purpose, and ministry priorities of a congregation; they must carry on with preaching, teaching, pastoring, overseeing, delegating, and so on. But seeking to more fully respect what their congregation is and what it ought to be doing, a process that takes significant time if done collaboratively, congregational leaders *can* work on building a culture of respect in their congregation as they carry on their regular ministry tasks. Unless preceded and accompanied by everyday ministry that is consistently respectful in its execution, the process of seeking clarity about congregational identity, purpose, and ministry priorities will turn out to be an unsatisfactory academic exercise.

To illustrate what respectful ministry looks like, I refer to Lowell Erdahl's *10 Habits for Effective Ministry*, mentioned in my introduction. It offers congregational leaders great wisdom, gained by a long life spent in pastoral ministry; in particular, Erdahl exudes respect, which I summarize as follows:

- Respect limitations: "We are all vulnerable . . . we have kinship with one another in our weakness . . . . In our trembling vulnerability we, like the apostle Paul, live by this promise: "My grace is sufficient for you, for my power is made perfect in weakness."[2]

---

2. Erdahl, *10 Habits*, 21–22.

Epilogue

- Respect God's grace: "Freed from having to struggle to lift ourselves up . . . let God's love hold us. Resting in that love, we are free to forget ourselves, and by the gracious energy God 'mightily inspires' within us to fulfill the life-giving ministry that is ours in Christ."[3]
- Respect congregants: "When a senior pastor encouraged a new associate to . . . visit with a group of elderly women meeting at the church, the young pastor replied, 'I don't have time.' To which the senior pastor replied, 'You should not only take time, but when you are there . . . take off your shoes because you are standing on holy ground.'"[4]
- Respect congregants: "Years ago, Paul Tournier expressed the conviction that we help people more by confessing our struggles and difficulties than by boasting of our strengths and victories. Sharing that does not violate boundaries, but acknowledges that we are in the struggle of life together, is a vital aspect of the compassion that creates bonding."[5]
- Respect lay leaders: "We evoke more gifts and mobilize more people by encouraging and affirming than by complaining and correcting . . . . Our basic business as Christian leaders is to build up, not tear down, to be constructors, not wreckers."[6]

I could continue, but I have quoted enough from Erdahl's first fifty pages to make my point—that the value of a culture of respect in congregations can hardly be overestimated. My own attempts at respectful congregational leadership often involved what I call "charitable assumption." The doctrine of charitable assumption goes like this: If a young couple not known to my congregation asks if I will marry them, I will charitably assume that what prompted that couple to ask for this was not the sanctuary's long, stately central aisle, but God's Spirit. Yes, a careful conversation will need to take place, but that conversation will be different if preceded by charitable assumption. Or how about a congregant who asks to meet me because she wants to express her disappointment in me. As I anticipate that visit, I will begin to build a wall of justification to defend myself from attack. After all, clergy-killers do exist. But what if I choose to charitably assume that the complainant has a legitimate case? I will be less defensive and more open to correction. As noted at the end of the previous chapter, there

3. Erdahl, *10 Habits*, 25.
4. Erdahl, *10 Habits*, 29.
5. Erdahl, *10 Habits*, 33.
6. Erdahl, *10 Habits*, 46–47.

are times when congregational leaders need to accept the pain that comes with the admission of faults and failures. But there is this: Our confession of fallibility is likely to build a more respectful congregational culture.

As I bring this book to a close, I am aware of all sorts of congregational issues not addressed. Take, for example, a congregation's governance style; the Presbyterian polity to which I adhere is one style choice. But no matter what the governance style, choices about its application and adaptation must still be made. As to worship, its form ought to respect and reflect what worship is and to whom it is being given, but again, choices remain to be made about worship style—will there be a choir or a praise group, an organ or guitars, hymnbooks or an overhead projector? Because so much congregational style revolves around what the Protestant Reformers referred to as *adiaphora*—choices that scripture neither endorses nor prohibits—respect is required as those choices are made, choices that will ensure that every congregation ends up being unique. That said, congregations ought not to be distracted from respecting their fundamental identity, purpose, and pattern of ministry.

Well, the word "respect" has certainly had a workout in my book and has quite possibly been overused, but it is, nevertheless, an important word for congregations. At its best, respect *within* congregations, respect *for* congregations, and respect *from* congregations help them to witness to the heart and mind of God, expressed in every aspect of the ministry of Jesus Christ. Our God is never casual or careless, neglectful, or dismissive; as Jesus said, not a sparrow falls "to the ground apart from your Father," and "even the hairs of your head are all counted" (Matt 10:29–30). If so, and that is Jesus's point, how much more will God take seriously and respect those made in God's image? God's people are called, individually and congregationally, to exercise a similar respect.

One final word: Jesus is at the core of respecting congregations because he is at the core of the Bible. The Bible presents a multitude of names for God, all of them valuable; but the most important is the name Jesus. Canadian homiletician Michael Knowles captures this in these words: "Those who have heard the Name are able to say with John the Evangelist, 'We have beheld his glory, full of grace and truth; we have seen him and heard him and some can even say they have touched him' (cf. John 1:14; 1 John 1:1)."[7] A congregation that keeps Jesus at its core is not guaranteed success, but it ought to be applauded for taking seriously, attending to, and respecting the One who defines what a Christian congregation is all about: Jesus.

---

7. Knowles, "I Will Proclaim," 205.

Bibliography

Alberta, Tim. *The Kingdom, the Power, and the Glory: American Evangelicals in an Age of Extremism*. New York: Harper, 2023.
Ammerman, Nancy T., et al., eds. *Studying Congregations: A New Handbook*. Nashville: Abingdon, 1998.
Anderson, Bernard W. *The Unfolding Drama of the Bible*. 4th ed. Minneapolis: Fortress, 2006.
Bainton, Roland H. *Here I Stand: A Life of Martin Luther*. Scarborough, ON: A Mentor Book, 1950.
Banks, Robert J. *Paul's Idea of Community: The Early House Churches in Their Cultural Settling*. Rev. ed. Peabody, MA: Hendrickson, 1994.
Barclay, William. *The Letters to the Corinthians*. Edinburgh: Saint Andrew, 1954.
Barnes, M. Craig. "The Post-Anxiety Church." *The Christian Century* 133.3 (Feb. 3, 2016). https://www.christiancentury.org/article/2016-01/post-anxiety-church.
Barth, Karl. *Church Dogmatics*. IV/2: *The Doctrine of Reconciliation*. Translated by G. W. Bromiley. Edinburgh: T & T Clark, 1958.
———. *Homiletics*. Louisville: Westminster/John Knox, 1991.
Beecher, Henry Ward. *Yale Lectures on Preaching, First Series*. Boston: Pilgrim, 1900.
Bell, John. "Reforming Worship: Change Is Not a Dirty Word." *Reformed Worship* 40 (June 1996) 5–11.
Blackwood, Andrew Watterson. *Pastoral Leadership*. Nashville: Abingdon-Cokesbury, 1949.
Bolsinger, Tod. *Canoeing the Mountains: Christian Leadership in Uncharted Territory*. Downers Grove, IL: InterVarsity, 2015.
Bruce, F. F. *1 and 2 Corinthians*. New Century Bible. London: Oliphants, 1971.
Burke, Edmund. *Reflections on the Revolution in France*. Repr., Bolton, ON: Amazon.ca, 2024.
Buttrick, David. *Homiletic: Moves and Structures*. Philadelphia: Fortress, 1987.
Calvin, John. *Calvin's Commentaries: The First Epistle of Paul to the Corinthians*. Edinburgh: St. Andrew, 1960.
Christian Reformed Church. "Yearbook and Online Data: Statistics 1963–Present." https://docs.google.com/spreadsheets/d/1oQamXOdPoL6AEs3WOCCZqbImu8SJIUCOIzpswny7Gx8/edit?gid=0#gid=0.

Bibliography

Clapp, Rodney. *Families at the Crossroads: Beyond Traditional and Modern Options.* Downers Grove, IL: InterVarsity, 1993.

Clarke, Brian, and Stuart Macdonald. *Leaving Christianity: Changing Allegiances in Canada Since 1945.* Montreal: McGill-Queens University Press, 2017.

Coggin, Donald. *The Sacrament of the Word.* London: Collins Fount, 1987.

Craddock, Fred B. *As One Without Authority.* St. Louis: Chalice, 2001.

———. *Preaching.* Burlington, ON: Welch, 1988.

———. "When the Roll Is Called Down Here." Preaching Today. https://www.preachingtoday.com/sermons/sermons/2010/july/whentherolliscalleddownhere.html.

Cranfield, C. E. B. *A Critical and Exegetical Commentary on the Epistle to the Romans.* Vol. 1. Edinburgh: T. & T. Clark, 1975.

Cullmann, Oscar. *The Christology of the New Testament.* London: SCM, 1959.

Dawn, Marva J. *A Royal "Waste" of Time: The Splendor of Worshiping God and Being Church for the World.* Grand Rapids: Eerdmans, 1999.

Dillon, Robin S. "Respect." *The Stanford Encyclopedia of Philosophy*, Fall 2022, edited by Edward N. Zalta and Uri Nodelman. https://plato.stanford.edu/archives/fall2022/entries/respect/.

Easum, William. *Dancing with Dinosaurs: Ministry in a Hostile and Hurting World.* Nashville: Abingdon, 1993.

———. *Leadership on the Other Side: No Rules, Just Clues.* Nashville: Abingdon, 2000.

Engel, Matthew. "1962: A Volcanic Year." *The Economist: 1843 Magazine*, Jan. 5, 2012. https://www.economist.com/1843/2012/01/05/1962-a-volcanic-year.

Erdahl, Lowell O. *10 Habits for Effective Ministry: A Guide for Life-Giving Pastors.* Minneapolis: Augsburg, 1996.

Ervine, Clyde. "Single in the Church: Eunuchs in the Kingdom." *Churchman* 119.3 (Autumn 2005) 217–32.

Farris, Stephen. *Preaching That Matters: The Bible and Our Lives.* Louisville: Westminster John Knox, 1998.

Finney, Mark T. *Honour and Conflict in the Ancient World: 1 Corinthians in Its Greco-Roman Social Setting.* London: T&T Clark, 2012.

Forsyth, P. T. *Positive Preaching and Modern Mind: The Lyman Beecher Lecture on Preaching, Yale University, Second Edition.* Eugene, OR: Wipf & Stock, 2008.

Fosdick, Harry Emerson. *The Living of These Days: An Autobiography.* New York: Harper & Brothers, 1956.

France, R. T. *Divine Government: God's Kingship in the Gospel of Mark.* London: SPCK, 1990.

Goheen, Michael W., and Craig G. Bartholomew. *The True Story of the Whole World: Finding Your Place in the Biblical Drama.* Grand Rapids: Faith Alive Christian Resources, 2009.

Grant, J. Webster. *The Canadian Experience of Church Union.* London: Lutterworth, 1967.

Green, Joel B. *1 Peter.* Two Horizons New Testament Commentary. Grand Rapids: Eerdmans, 2007.

Guder, Darrell L. *Called to Witness: Doing Missional Theology.* Grand Rapids: Eerdmans, 2015.

———. "Missional Church: From Sending to Being Sent." In *Missional Church: A Vision for the Sending of the Church in North America*, edited by Darrell L. Guder. Grand Rapids: Eerdmans, 1998.

———. "Missional Structures: The Particular Community." In *Missional Church: A Vision for the Sending of the Church in North America*, edited by Darrell L. Guder. Grand Rapids: Eerdmans, 1998.
Hauerwas, Stanley. *A Better Hope: Resources for a Church Confronting Capitalism, Democracy, and Postmodernity*. Grand Rapids: Brazos, 2000.
Hays, Richard B. *First Corinthians*. Interpretation: A Bible Commentary for Teaching and Preaching. Louisville: John Knox, 1997.
Henkin, Louis, ed. *The International Bill of Rights*. New York: Columbia University Press, 1981.
Hoon, Paul Waitman. *The Integrity of Worship: Ecumenical and Pastoral Studies in Liturgical Theology*. Nashville: Abingdon, 1971.
Hudson, Alexandra. *The Soul of Civility: Timeless Principles to Heal Society and Ourselves*. New York: St. Martin's, 2023.
Hunsberger, George. "Missional Vocation: Called and Sent to Represent the Reign of God." In *Missional Church: A Vision for the Sending of the Church in North America*, edited by Darrell L. Guder. Grand Rapids: Eerdmans, 1998.
Jacobs, Jane. *The Death and Life of Great American Cities*. New York: Vintage Random House, 1992.
Jenkins, Philip. *The Next Christendom: The Coming of Global Christianity*. New York: Oxford University Press, 2007.
Kant, Immanuel. *The Metaphysics of Ethics*. 5th ed. Translated by J. W. Semple. Edinburgh: T. & T. Clark, 1869.
Kelley, Dean M. *Why Conservative Churches Are Growing: A Study in Sociology of Religion*. New York: Harper & Row, 1972.
Kincaid, Paula R. "EPC Continues to Grow in 2016." *The Layman*, June 14, 2017. https://layman.org/epc-continues-grow-2016/.
Knowles, Michael P. "I Will Proclaim the Name [Exodus 34:6–9] [1996]." In *The Folly of Preaching: Models and Methods*, edited by Michael P. Knowles. Grand Rapids: Eerdmans, 2007.
Leith, John H. *Basic Christian Doctrine*. Louisville: Westminster/John Knox, 1993.
Lewis, C. S. *Reflections on the Psalms*. London: Collins, 1958.
Long, Thomas G. *Beyond the Worship Wars: Building Vital and Faithful Worship*. Herndon, VA: Alban Institute, 2001.
———. "Taking the Listeners Seriously as the People of God." In *The Folly of Preaching: Models and Methods*, edited by Michael P. Knowles. Grand Rapids: Eerdmans, 2007.
———. *The Witness of Preaching*. Louisville: Westminster/John Knox, 1989.
Mackay, John A. *God's Order: The Ephesian Letter and This Present Time*. New York: MacMillan, 1953.
Martin, Ralph P. *Worship in the Early Church*. Grand Rapids: Eerdmans, 1974.
Mays, James Luther. *Psalms: Interpretation: A Bible Commentary for Teaching and Preaching*. Louisville: John Knox, 2011.
McCullough, Donald W. *The Trivialization of God: The Dangerous Illusion of a Manageable Deity*. Colorado Springs: Navpress, 1995.
McGavran, Donald A. *Understanding Church Growth*. Rev. ed. Grand Rapids: Eerdmans, 1970.
McGavran, Donald A., and Winfield C. Arn. *Ten Steps for Church Growth*. New York: HarperCollins, 1977.

Bibliography

McGrath, Alister. *Mere Theology: Christian Faith and the Discipleship of the Mind*. London: SPCK, 2010.

McKnight, Scot. "Church History and Lessons/Warnings from the Church Growth of Willow Creek Community Church." *Christianity Today*, Oct. 4, 2020. https://churchhealthwiki.wordpress.com/2020/10/05/church-history-lessons-warnings-from-the-church-growth-of-willow-creek-community-church-scotmcknight/.

———. *Kingdom Conspiracy: Returning to the Radical Mission of the Local Church*. Grand Rapids: Brazos, 2014.

———. "Willow Creek's Troubles Can Be Found in Its Word Cloud." *Religion News Service*, Sept. 19, 2019. https://religionnews.com/2019/09/19/willow-creeks-troubles-can-be-found-in-its-word-cloud/.

McKnight, Scot, and Laura Barringer. *A Church Called Tov: Forming a Goodness Culture That Resists Abuses of Power*. Carol Stream, IL: Tyndale Momentum, 2020.

McLelland, Joseph C. *Understanding the Faith: Essays in Philosophical Theology*. Toronto: Clements Academic, 2007.

Mead, Loren B. *The Once and Future Church: Reinventing the Congregation for a New Mission Frontier*. Herndon, VA: Alban Institute, 1991.

Michaelsen, Robert. "The Protestant Ministry in America: 1850 to the Present." In *The Ministry in Historical Perspective*, edited by H. Richard Niebuhr and Daniel D. Williams. New York: Harper and Brothers, 1956.

Mitchell, Margaret M. *Paul and the Rhetoric of Reconciliation: An Exegetical Investigation of the Language and Composition of 1 Corinthians*. Louisville: Westminster/John Knox, 1992.

Morris, Leon. *I Believe in Revelation*. Grand Rapids: Eerdmans, 1976.

Mouw, Richard J. *Uncommon Decency: Christian Civility in an Uncivil World*. 2nd ed. Downers Grove, IL: InterVarsity, 2010.

Mulder, Mark T. *Congregations, Neighborhoods, Places*. Grand Rapids: Calvin College Press, 2018.

Neill, Stephen. *A History of Christian Missions*. Hammondsworth, England: Penguin, 1964.

———. *The Interpretation of the New Testament 1861–1961*. London: Oxford University Press, 1966.

Newbigin, Lesslie. *The Gospel in a Pluralist Society*. Grand Rapids: Eerdmans, 1989.

———. *The Household of God: Lectures on the Nature of the Church*. London: SCM, 1957.

———. *Sign of the Kingdom*. Grand Rapids: Eerdmans, 1981.

Nicholson, Adam. *God's Secretaries: The Making of the King James Bible*. New York: Harper Perennial, 2005.

Nicole, Roger. "Warfield, Benjamin Breckinridge [1851–1921]." In *Encyclopedia of the Reformed Faith*, edited by Donald K. McKim. Louisville: Westminster/John Knox, 1992.

Osborne, Robert. "Spiritual Leadership as Representative." Unpublished manuscript, 2005.

Our Confessional Heritage: Confessions of the Reformed Tradition with a Contemporary Declaration of Faith. Atlanta: The General Assembly of the Presbyterian Church in the United States, 1978.

Page, Nick. *And Now Let's Move into a Time of Nonsense: Why Worship Songs Are Failing the Church*. Milton Keynes, UK: Authentic Media, 2004.

Parker, T. H. L. *John Calvin*. Berkhamsted, Hertfordshire: Lion, 1975.

Bibliography

———. *Portrait of Calvin*. London: SCM, 1954.
Percy, Harold. *Good News People: An Introduction to Evangelism for Tongue-Tied Christians*. Toronto: Anglican Book Centre, 1996.
———. *Your Church Can Thrive: Making the Connections That Build Healthy Congregations*. Toronto: Anglican Book Centre, 2003.
Perry, Abby. "Willow Creek and Harvest Struggle to Move On." *Christianity Today*, Feb. 13, 2020. https://www.christianitytoday.com/2020/02/willow-creek-harvest-after-hybels-macdonald-moving-on/.
Peterson, Eugene H. *Run with the Horses: The Quest for Life at Its Best*. Downers Grove, IL: InterVarsity, 1983.
———. *Working the Angles: The Shape of Pastoral Integrity*. Grand Rapids: Eerdmans, 1987.
Presbyterian Church in Canada. *The Book of Common Worship*. Presbyterian Church in Canada, 1991.
———. *The Book of Praise*. Toronto: Oxford University Press, 1918.
———. *Living Faith: A Statement of Christian Belief*. Kelowna, BC: Wood Lake Publishing, 1984.
———. "New Beginnings." https://presbyterian.ca/canadian-ministries/new-beginnings/.
Purves, Andrew. *Reconstructing Pastoral Theology: A Christological Foundation*. Louisville: Westminster John Knox, 2004.
Quinley, Harold. *The Prophetic Clergy: Social Activism Among Protestant Ministers*. New York: John Wiley & Sons, 1974.
Read, David H. C. *Sent from God: The Enduring Power and Mystery of Preaching*. Nashville: Abingdon, 1974.
Richardson, Kurt Anders. "The Contemporary Renewal of Trinitarian Theology: Possibilities of Convergence in the Doctrine of God." In *The Nature of Confession: Evangelicals and Postliberals in Conversation*, edited by Timothy R. Phillips and Dennis L. Okholm. Downers Grove, IL: InterVarsity, 1996.
Robinson, Anthony B. *Transforming Congregational Culture*. Grand Rapids: Eerdmans, 2003.
Root, Andrew, and Blair D. Bertrand. *When Church Stops Working: A Future for Your Congregation Beyond More Money, Programs, and Innovations*. Grand Rapids: Brazos, 2023.
Roxburgh, Alan J. *Joining God, Remaking Church, Changing the World: The New Shape of the Church in Our Time*. New York: Morehouse, 2015.
Schaller, Lyle E. *44 Ways to Increase Church Attendance*. Nashville: Abingdon, 1988.
———. *The Change Agent: The Strategy of Innovative Leadership*. Nashville: Abingdon, 1972.
Schowalter, Daniel N. "Church." In *The Oxford Companion to the Bible*, edited by Bruce M. Metzger and Michael D. Coogan. New York: Oxford University Press, 1993.
Shellnutt, Kate. "SBC Membership Falls to 47-Year Low, But Church Involvement Is Up." *Christianity Today*, May 7, 2024. https://www.christianitytoday.com/2024/05/southern-baptist-church-decline-sbc-annual-church-profile/.
Smart, James D. *The Rebirth of Ministry: A Study in the Character of the Church's Ministry*. Philadelphia: Westminster, 1960.
———. *The Strange Silence of the Bible in the Church*. London: SCM, 1970.

Bibliography

St. Andrew's Presbyterian Church, NOTL. "Thanksgiving Sunday, October 8, 2023—Who Is This? The One Who Sets Us Free!" YouTube video, Oct. 8, 2023. https://www.youtube.com/watch?v=fEcJW2h6dUM.

Stevenson, J., ed. *Creeds, Councils, and Controversies*. London: SPCK, 1966.

———. *A New Eusebius*. London: SPCK, 1957.

Stott, John R. W. *Christian Mission in the Modern World: What the Church Should Be Doing Now*. Downers Grove, IL: InterVarsity, 1975.

———. *I Believe in Preaching*. Toronto: Hodder and Stoughton, 1982.

Thiselton, Anthony C. *First Corinthians: A Shorter Exegetical and Pastoral Commentary*. Grand Rapids: Eerdmans, 2006.

———. *The First Epistle to the Corinthians: A Commentary on the Greek Text*. Grand Rapids: Eerdmans, 2000.

Torrance, James B. *Worship, Community and the Triune God of Grace*. Downers Grove, IL: InterVarsity, 1996.

Trench, Richard Chenevix. *Notes on the Parables of Our Lord, Eleventh Edition*. New York: D. Appleton and Company, 1902.

Tuhus-Dubrow, Rebecca. "An Ad Hoc Affair." *The Nation*, Feb. 3, 2017. https://www.thenation.com/article/archive/jane-jacobss-radical-vision-of-humanity/.

Van Gelder, Craig. *The Essence of the Church: A Community Created by the Spirit*. Grand Rapids: Baker, 2000.

Van Gelder, Craig, and Dwight J. Zscheile. *Participating in God's Mission: A Theological Missiology for the Church in America*. Grand Rapids: Eerdmans, 2018.

Vissers, John A. *The Neo-Orthodox Theology of W. W. Bryden*. Eugene, OR: Pickwick, 2006.

Webster, Douglas D. *Selling Jesus: What's Wrong with Marketing the Church*. Downers Grove, IL: InterVarsity, 1992.

Willimon, William H. "Baptismal Speech." In *The Company of Preachers: Wisdom on Preaching, Augustine to the Present*, edited by Richard Lischer. Grand Rapids: Eerdmans, 2002.

Wright, Christopher J. H. *The Mission of God's People: A Biblical Theology of the Church's Mission*. Grand Rapids: Zondervan, 2010.

Wright, N. T. *The Day the Revolution Began: Reconsidering the Meaning of Jesus's Crucifixion*. New York: HarperOne, 2016.

———. *Paul for Everyone: The Prison Letters*. London: SPCK Westminster John Knox, 2004.

———. *Scripture and the Authority of God: How to Read the Bible Today*. New York: HarperOne, 2011.

———. *Simply Good News: Why the Gospel Is News and What Makes It Good*. New York: HarperOne, 2015.

www.ingramcontent.com/pod-product-compliance
Lightning Source LLC
Chambersburg PA
CBHW072153160426
43197CB00012B/2372